Protection Gaps in Insurance for Natural Hazards and Retirement Savings in Asia

OECD

BETTER POLICIES FOR BETTER LIVES

Please cite this publication as:
OECD (2025), *Protection Gaps in Insurance for Natural Hazards and Retirement Savings in Asia*, OECD Publishing, Paris, https://doi.org/10.1787/294f044e-en.

ISBN 978-92-64-74912-2 (print)
ISBN 978-92-64-78584-7 (PDF)
ISBN 978-92-64-94818-1 (HTML)

Photo credits: Cover © imtmphoto/Getty Images.

Corrigenda to OECD publications may be found at: https://www.oecd.org/en/publications/support/corrigenda.html.

Foreword

Individuals encounter various risks throughout their lives for which they may not be adequately protected. Two significant risks that can impact an individual's financial well-being relate to natural hazards and the transition from working life to retirement. Insurance and asset-backed pensions offer protection against these risks. However, individuals may sometimes be unable or unwilling to utilise these protections, either due to personal choice or a lack of available vehicles and options. This situation may result in financial protection gaps, leaving individuals vulnerable and potentially jeopardising their financial well-being.

This report identifies and addresses financial protection gaps in insurance for natural hazards and retirement savings in Asia. It provides an overview of these gaps in Asia, assesses the drivers and provides approaches to addressing these gaps based on international good practices. The analysis focuses on the experiences of Indonesia, Malaysia, Pakistan, the Philippines and Sri Lanka (insurance and retirement savings), as well as Thailand and Viet Nam (retirement savings only). The report also draws from the work of the OECD Working Party on Insurance and Pensions, contributing to the dissemination of OECD standards and recommendations relating to insurance and asset-backed pensions.

This report was prepared by the Capital Markets and Financial Institutions Division of the OECD Directorate for Financial and Enterprise Affairs under the supervision of Pablo Antolín, Head of the Insurance and Pensions Unit, and Serdar Çelik, Head of Division. Chapter 1 was prepared by Leigh Wolfrom, with support from Timothy Bishop, and Chapter 2 was prepared by Stéphanie Payet and Jessica Mosher. The information gathered in this report was collected through desk research, questionnaires and discussions with relevant stakeholders in the participating countries.

The OECD gratefully acknowledges financial support from the Government of Japan. The report also benefitted from valuable exchanges and collaboration with the Financial Services Authority (Indonesia); Bank Negara Malaysia and the Employee Provident Fund (Malaysia); the Securities and Exchange Commission of Pakistan (Pakistan); the Insurance Commission and the Social Security System (the Philippines); the Insurance Regulatory Commission of Sri Lanka and the Employees' Provident Fund (Sri Lanka); the Fiscal Policy Office and the Government Pension Fund (Thailand); the Ministry of Home Affairs (Viet Nam); and representatives from the private (re)insurance and pensions sector in all these countries.

Table of contents

FIGURES

TABLES

BOXES

Executive summary

Asian countries face significant financial protection gaps in natural hazard insurance and retirement savings, leaving individuals under-protected and putting their financial well-being at risk. This report examines the drivers of these gaps and identifies possible approaches to addressing them, focusing on the experiences of Indonesia, Malaysia, Pakistan, the Philippines, Sri Lanka, Thailand and Viet Nam.

Protection gaps in natural hazard insurance are the result of factors that limit the demand and supply of insurance coverage.

The take-up of insurance coverage for natural hazard risks remains low across Asia, despite relatively high levels of awareness and perception of natural hazard risks. This is driven by a limited understanding of the need for and benefits of insurance coverage to protect against these risks and a lack of trust in insurance. Differences in insurers' approach to offering natural hazard insurance coverage may also lead to misunderstandings about the availability of coverage or the need to acquire specific additional coverage. For lower-income segments of the population and those in high-risk areas, insurance coverage may simply be unaffordable.

Insurers may also face constraints to their appetite and/or capacity to provide coverage to households and businesses for natural hazard risks. Limited access to quality data and risk assessment tools such as catastrophe models can inhibit insurers' ability to quantify the potential frequency and severity of losses, as well as their ability to price premiums based on risk. In some countries, intensive competition and price-sensitive consumers may be discouraging insurers from charging higher premiums in higher risk areas and leading them to impose higher deductibles, limit the sums insured or exclude coverage for some or all natural hazard risks. Challenges in quantifying natural hazard risk and ensuring adequate pricing have also led to some difficulties in accessing affordable reinsurance coverage, thereby further reducing the appetite of insurers for providing coverage for natural hazard risks to households and businesses.

Increasing the demand for natural hazard insurance coverage will require actions to:

- Improve insurance literacy and increase trust in insurance companies and insurance coverage as an effective form of financial protection.
- Augment property insurance penetration by expanding the use of digital distribution channels and bancassurance, and by encouraging the development of suitable and affordable insurance coverage products.
- Expand the take-up of natural hazard coverage by encouraging insurers to improve consistency and clarity on coverage and exclusions, and by considering the advantages and disadvantages of requiring insurers to offer natural hazard coverage automatically in property insurance coverage.

Ensuring the availability of affordable insurance coverage for natural hazard risks will require efforts to:

- Improve access to quality data and modelling tools.

- Enhance the ability of insurers to adequately price coverage for natural hazard insurance and the capacity of insurance supervisors to oversee pricing adequacy and fairness.
- Support sustainable access to affordable reinsurance capacity, including through capital markets and by leveraging the contribution of national reinsurers.
- Consider the potential benefits of establishing public-private insurance programmes.

Protection gaps in retirement savings result from the lack of participation in pension schemes, and when individuals do participate, from insufficient pension benefits that may not cover them for their entire lifetime in retirement.

The participation of working-age individuals in mandatory and voluntary pension schemes is low in most of the countries analysed. Several factors contribute to this. First, most mandatory pension schemes only cover formal employees. Due to low labour force participation rates, particularly among women, and widespread informality, many individuals are left without access to mandatory pension schemes. In addition, certain employers, in particular smaller ones, may be exempted from registering their employees, while others do not comply with their obligation to do so. Second, the availability of voluntary pension schemes may be limited because few employers and providers offer access to occupational and personal pension plans. Third, individuals may not make use of the existing vehicles to save for retirement because of a lack of awareness of the need to save for retirement and of the different products available to them, a lack of financial incentives, or a lack of affordability.

The retirement income that individuals participating in the pension system can expect to receive may not always be adequate. Short contribution periods, in particular due to low retirement ages, and the possibility to withdraw savings before retirement, are the two main drivers of lower-than-expected pension benefits from defined contribution pension schemes. Moreover, restrictive investment limits and conservative investment strategies expose pension funds to concentration risk and may lead to lower performance in the long term. Defined benefit pension schemes may provide adequate retirement benefits to those fulfilling all the requirements, but a combination of high service period requirements and lack of portability between different pension schemes may reduce the share of members eventually entitled to pension benefits. In addition, contributions may not be reflective of expected benefits, leading either to a lack of incentives to contribute or to increased risks to sustainability. Lastly, many retiring individuals may lack protection from longevity risk.

Addressing financial protection gaps in retirement savings requires a range of measures to better align the rules of the pension systems with their objectives, enhance the availability of savings and retirement income vehicles, and expand their take-up by individuals. This includes to:

- Expand the coverage of mandatory pension schemes, implement automatic enrolment for voluntary pension schemes, and improve financial incentives and financial literacy on pensions to increase participation rates.
- Align contribution levels with expected benefits and increase contribution periods, in particular by extending retirement ages.
- Provide investment choice to members with appropriate default options and improve portfolio diversification.
- Improve the portability of pension entitlements.
- Limit early withdrawals of retirement savings to exceptional hardship circumstances.
- Design payout options in line with people's needs in retirement, in particular by ensuring the availability of lifetime retirement income solutions.

1 Protection gaps in insurance for natural hazards

This chapter examines the drivers of protection gaps in natural hazard insurance in Asia and possible approaches to addressing these gaps. It provides an overview of exposure to natural hazard risk in emerging and developing Asia and Pacific countries and the magnitude of protection gaps; outlines the main drivers of protection gaps in this region; and discusses possible policy, regulatory, supervisory and market approaches to addressing protection gaps in natural hazard insurance.

There are significant "protection gaps" in insurance for natural hazard risks in many countries, particularly in emerging markets and developing countries. Natural hazards such as floods, earthquakes and cyclones can lead to significant damage to buildings and infrastructure, and losses of revenues and income linked to economic disruptions. The damages and losses resulting from these types of relatively infrequent but large-scale events have generally been challenging to insure as households and businesses will often underestimate the need for financial protection and as insurers may be reluctant to provide coverage for large-scale, correlated and uncertain risks.

Protection gaps can burden households and businesses with losses that they are unable to absorb, and recovery and rebuilding needs that they are unable to fund. Insufficient funding can slow recovery and reconstruction and prolong economic disruption, increasing the ultimate cost. Protection gaps can also create pressures on public finances as a result of a reduction in revenues linked to economic activity and an increase in expenditures linked to recovery and reconstruction. There could also be implications for financial stability if uninsured damages and losses lead to widespread defaults on outstanding loans and mortgages.

An increase in the frequency and/or intensity of many types of natural hazards could exacerbate protection gaps leading to larger and more regular losses. Increased losses could force insurance and reinsurance companies to charge more for the coverage they provide, making insurance coverage less or un-affordable for an increasing share of the population.

This chapter examines the drivers of protection gaps in natural hazard insurance and possible approaches to addressing these gaps, with a focus on Asia.[1] Asia is one of the regions most exposed to natural hazards and vulnerable to climate risks.[2] The chapter examines protection gaps in natural hazard insurance for households and businesses specifically, and does not consider the role of insurance markets in providing financial protection to governments or public assets[3], nor does it examine disaster risk reduction or climate adaptation, beyond noting their important contribution to supporting insurability and reducing protection gaps.

The first section provides an overview of the exposure to natural hazard risk in Asian countries and the magnitude of protection gaps. The second section outlines the main drivers of protection gaps in insurance for natural hazard risks in this region. The third section discusses possible policy, regulatory, supervisory and market approaches to addressing protection gaps in natural hazard insurance. A final section provides some conclusions.

1.1. Natural hazards and protection gaps

Emerging and developing Asia and Pacific countries are exposed to a broad range of natural hazards, including earthquakes, floods, cyclones, convective storms and wildfires.[4] Between 2000 and 2023, natural hazards have led to annual average losses of approximately USD 48.4 billion across the region, driven by floods (46% of losses), earthquakes (23%) and cyclones (22%) (Figure 1.1).

Figure 1.1. Average annual economic losses by hazard and subregion (2000-23)

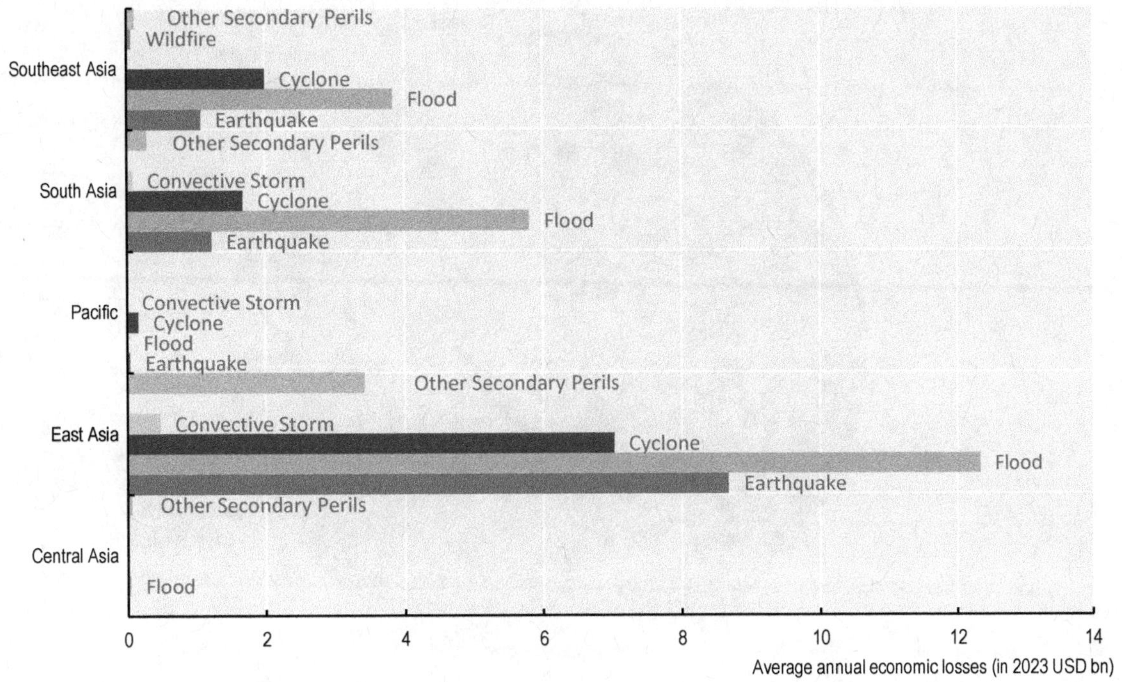

Note: Southeast Asia includes losses reported in Cambodia, Indonesia, Lao People's Democratic Republic, Malaysia, Myanmar, the Philippines, Thailand, Timor-Leste and Viet Nam. South Asia includes losses reported in Afghanistan, Bangladesh, Bhutan, India, the Maldives, Nepal, Pakistan and Sri Lanka. Pacific includes losses reported in Fiji, the Marshall Islands, Micronesia, Papua New Guinea, Samoa, the Solomon Islands, Tonga, Tuvalu and Vanuatu. East Asia includes losses reported in the People's Republic of China, the Democratic People's Republic of Korea and Mongolia. Central Asia includes losses reported in Kazakhstan, Kyrgyzstan and Tajikistan. No economic losses were reported in other countries during this period. "Other secondary perils" includes droughts and landslides.
Source: OECD calculations based on data provided by Swiss Re (Swiss Re, sigma database. All rights reserved.).

Countries classified as Upper Middle Income or Lower Middle Income incurred most of the reported losses, 75.7% and 24.2%, respectively. This reflects higher asset values, and potentially data gaps in lower income countries.[5] Twelve emerging and developing Asia and Pacific countries accounted for practically all (98.9%) of the reported losses (Figure 1.2).

Figure 1.2. Economic losses by country (2000-23, cumulative)

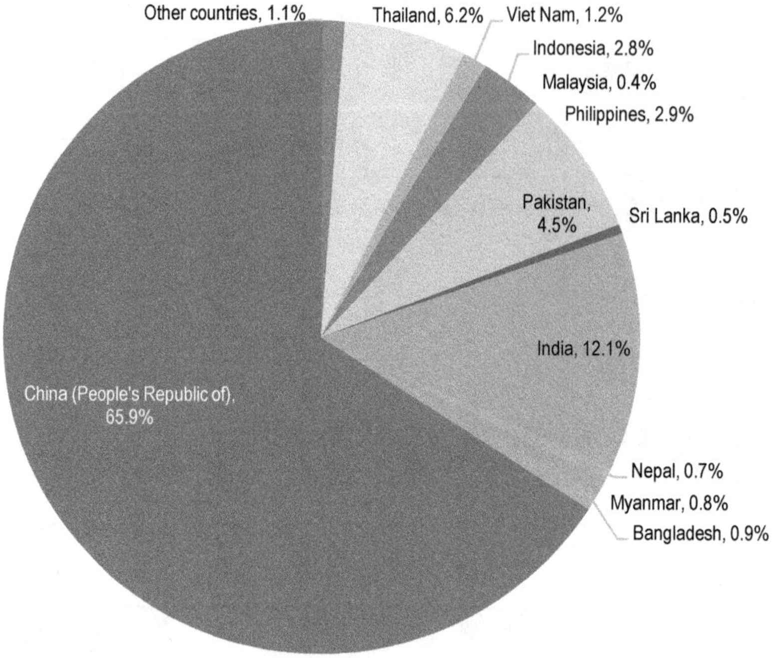

Source: OECD calculations based on data provided by Swiss Re (Swiss Re, sigma database. All rights reserved.).

Average annual economic losses from natural hazards were 165% higher in the most recent five-year period (2019-23) relative to the first five years of the century (2000-2004), driven by a significant increase in losses resulting from weather-related natural hazards. Average annual economic losses from weather-related losses increased from USD 10.8 billion (2000-2004) to USD 42.4 billion (2019-2023) (Figure 1.3).

Figure 1.3. Economic losses by hazard (2000-23, emerging and developing Asia and Pacific)

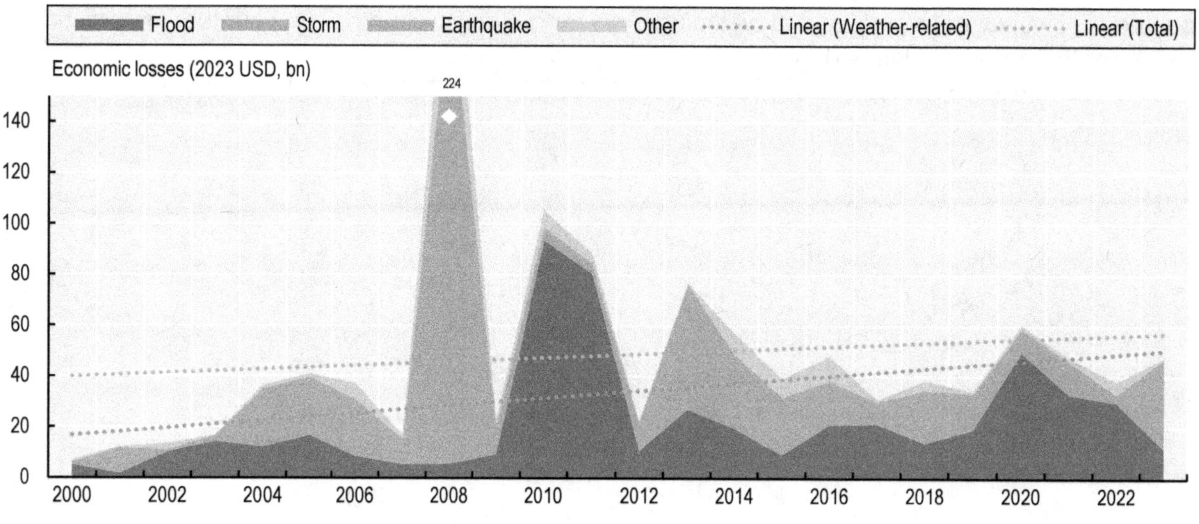

Note: "Other" includes wildfire, convective storms, droughts and landslides.
Source: OECD calculations based on data provided by Swiss Re (Swiss Re, sigma database. All rights reserved.).

There is an expectation that the frequency and intensity of many natural hazards across the region is going to increase. Flood risk could increase as a result of a projected large increase in annual precipitation across North, South and East Asia; more frequent heavy and intense precipitation episodes across South, Southeast and East Asia and the Pacific; an increase in precipitation accompanying tropical cyclones; sea-level rise in coastal areas; and the potential for glacial lake outburst floods in the Hindu Kush Himalaya region (Figure 1.4) (Shaw et al., 2023[1]). Wind and flood damage from tropical cyclones could increase due to an increase in the frequency of intense tropical cyclones in the western North Pacific (Shaw et al., 2023[1]). A number of emerging and developing Asia and Pacific countries are ranked among the countries most exposed[6] to significant climate change, including Bangladesh, India, Indonesia, the Democratic People's Republic of Korea, the Maldives, Myanmar, Pakistan, Papua New Guinea, the Philippines, Sri Lanka, Timor-Leste, , Viet Nam and a number of small island states (Kiribati, the Marshall Islands, Micronesia, Nauru, Palau, the Solomon Islands, Tonga, Tuvalu and Vanuatu) (Chen et al., 2025[2]).

Figure 1.4. Projected impact of climate change on natural hazards in Asia

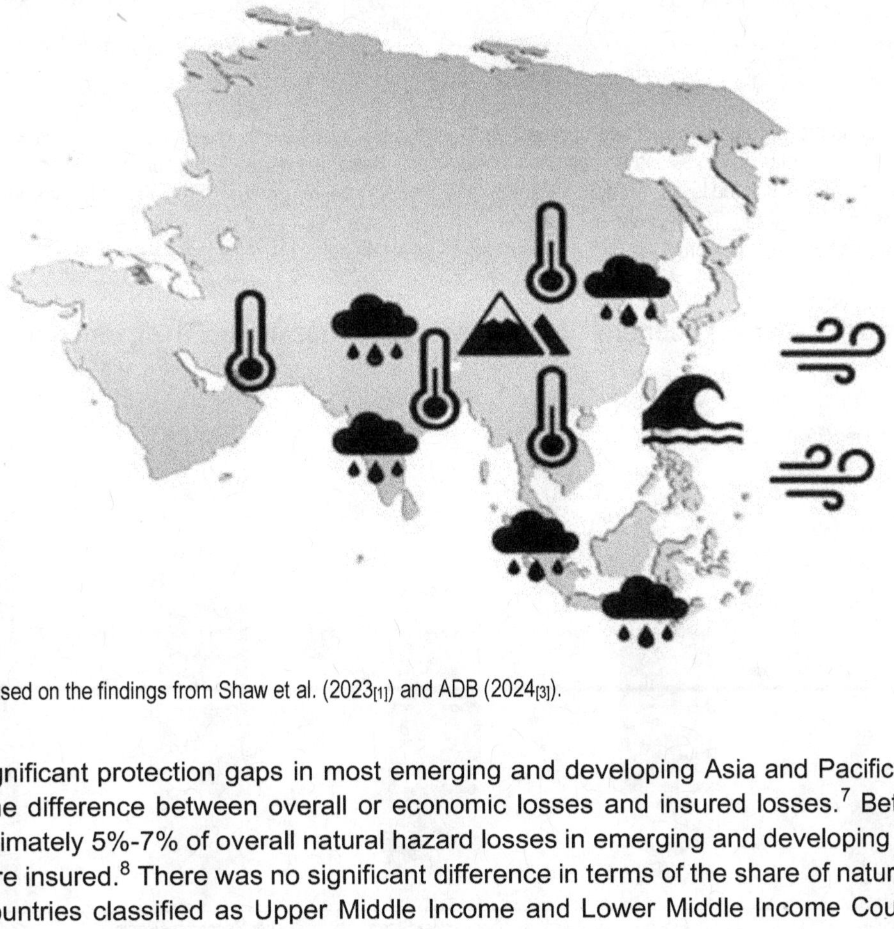

Source: OECD based on the findings from Shaw et al. (2023[1]) and ADB (2024[3]).

There are significant protection gaps in most emerging and developing Asia and Pacific countries, often defined as the difference between overall or economic losses and insured losses.[7] Between 2000 and 2023, approximately 5%-7% of overall natural hazard losses in emerging and developing Asia and Pacific countries were insured.[8] There was no significant difference in terms of the share of natural hazard losses insured in countries classified as Upper Middle Income and Lower Middle Income Countries[9] although there were substantial differences across individual countries (Figure 1.5). The estimated share of losses insured was below 5% in just over half of the countries examined.

There were also some differences in the share of losses insured among the different types of natural hazards. The share of earthquake losses insured was significantly lower than other types of natural hazards (Figure 1.6).

Figure 1.5. Estimated share of economic losses insured by country (2000-23)

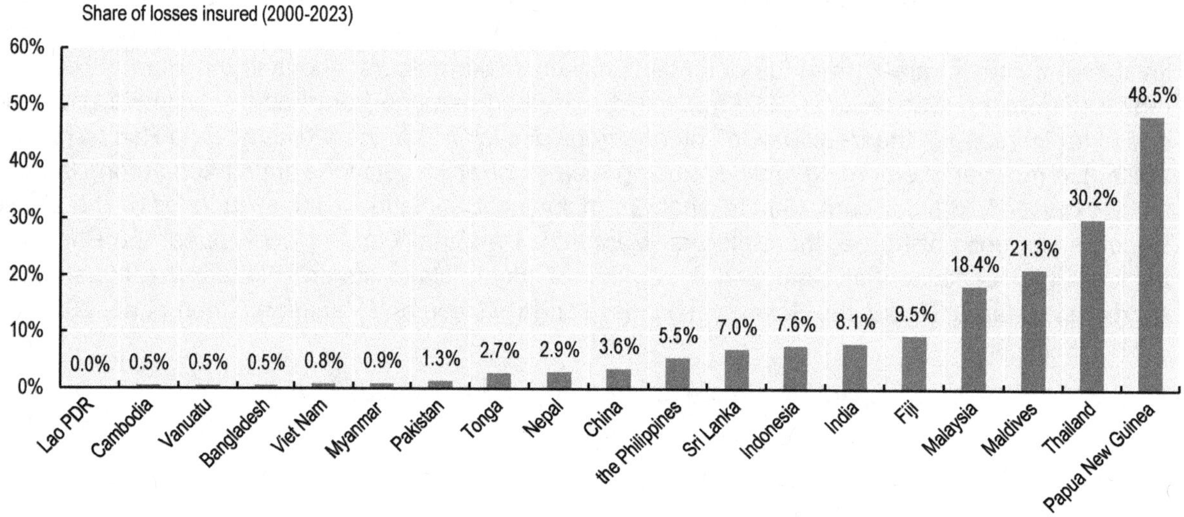

Note: The reported value is the average between two approaches to measuring the share of losses insured (i.e. an approach including all available data on insured and economic losses and an approach including only loss years where both insured and economic loss estimates are provided). There were no reported insured losses in Afghanistan, Bhutan, Kazakhstan, Kyrgyzstan, the Marshall Islands, Micronesia, Mongolia, Samoa, the Solomon Islands, Tajikistan, Timor-Leste or Tuvalu.
Source: OECD calculations based on data provided by Swiss Re (Swiss Re, sigma database. All rights reserved.).

Figure 1.6. Estimated share of economic losses insured by hazard (2000-23, emerging and developing Asia and Pacific)

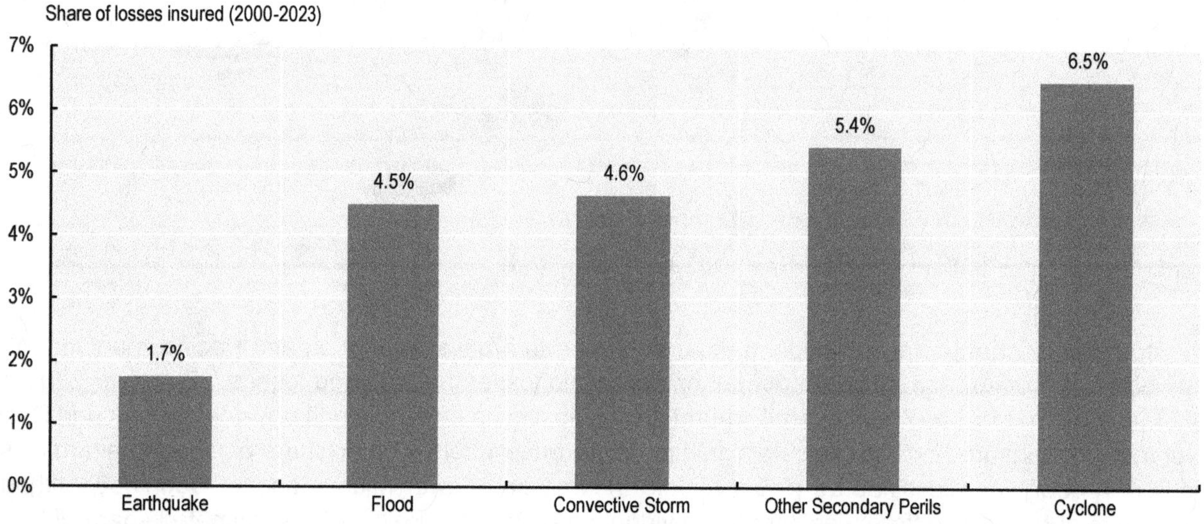

Note: The reported value is the average between two approaches to measuring the share of losses insured (i.e. an approach including all available data on insured and economic losses and an approach including only loss years where both insured and economic loss estimates are provided). "Other secondary perils" includes wildfire, droughts and landslides (although there were no reported losses from wildfires). Insured and economic losses due to floods in Thailand in 2011 were excluded above given the magnitude of the event and relatively high level of insured losses. Including those losses would lead to an estimate of 8.1% of flood losses that were insured.
Source: OECD calculations based on data provided by Swiss Re (Swiss Re, sigma database. All rights reserved.).

There has been some progress in reducing protection gaps across the region (Figure 1.7). In 2014-23, 6.6% of economic losses were insured, up from 2.6% in 2000-09.

Figure 1.7. Share of economic losses insured (2000-23, emerging and developing Asia and Pacific)

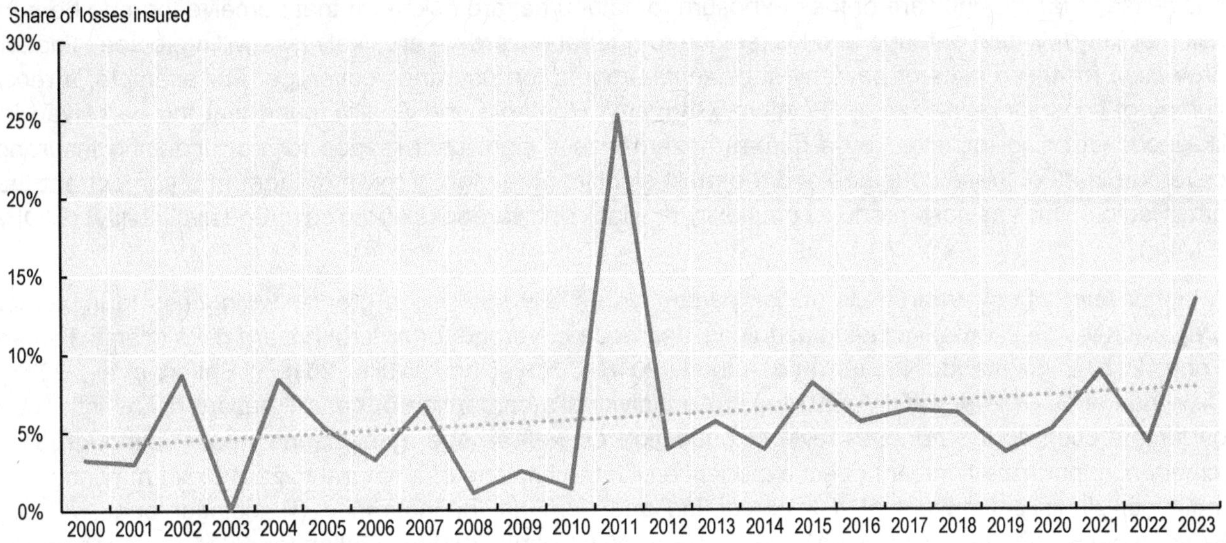

Note: The reported value is the average between two approaches to measuring the share of losses insured (i.e. an approach including all available data on insured and economic losses and an approach including only loss years where both insured and economic loss estimates are provided).
Source: OECD calculations based on data provided by Swiss Re (Swiss Re, sigma database. All rights reserved.).

1.2. Drivers of protection gaps in natural hazard insurance

Several factors that affect the demand for and supply of insurance coverage drive the limited insurance coverage of losses resulting from natural hazards. Limited demand reduces the amount that households and businesses will be willing to pay for natural hazard insurance coverage or their willingness to purchase any coverage at all. Limited supply reduces the amount of coverage that insurance companies are willing to offer or leads them to charge higher premiums. The gap between the demand for coverage and the supply of coverage drives protection gaps. The following sections outline the factors that could limit households' and businesses' willingness-to-pay for insurance coverage for natural hazard risks and the factors that could limit insurance companies' willingness to offer such coverage.

1.2.1. Factors that limit the willingness-to-pay for natural hazard insurance coverage – demand factors

Several factors impact the demand for natural hazard insurance coverage, including the level of awareness among households and businesses of their exposure to natural hazard risks and the availability and benefits of – and need for – specific coverage to protect against these risks. Households and businesses that do not perceive themselves to be at risk of being impacted by natural hazards or are unaware of the need for insurance coverage are less likely to acquire such insurance coverage. Households and small businesses with limited income or revenue may not have the financial capacity to allocate any significant amount of their spending towards insurance premiums for natural hazard insurance coverage. Insurance companies, intermediaries and regulators in Indonesia, Malaysia, Pakistan, the Philippines and Sri Lanka identified some or all of these factors as drivers of protection gaps in insurance for natural hazards during meetings and/or in their responses to a survey circulated for the development of this chapter.

Limited awareness of exposure to natural hazard risks

Limited awareness among households and businesses of their exposure to natural hazard risk and the potential damages or losses that they could face should they be impacted by a natural hazard is likely to affect the demand or willingness-to-pay for natural hazard insurance coverage. Households and businesses that are unaware of their exposure to natural hazard risks – or that perceive there to be a low risk that they will face damage and losses due to natural hazards – are likely less willing to seek financial protection for these risks or pay any substantial amount for insurance coverage. For example, a recent survey of consumers in Europe (Belgium, Germany, Romania and Spain) found that the perceived low likelihood of being impacted by a natural hazard was a significant reason for not acquiring insurance coverage in all of these countries and the most significant reason in three of them (more important than other factors, such as cost, product complexity or a lack of awareness about coverage availability) (EIOPA, 2024[4]).

A higher level of risk awareness or risk perception usually leads to a greater willingness to implement preparedness measures, including acquiring insurance coverage for natural hazard risks (Yang, Tan and Peng, 2020[5]; Reynaud, Nguyen and Aubert, 2018[6]; Royal and Walls, 2019[7]; Seifert et al., 2013[8]; Cisternas et al., 2024[9]; EIOPA, 2024[4]).[10] An individual's perception of natural hazard risk is influenced by factors such as the person's level of education as well as age, gender and wealth, although direct experience, particularly recent direct experience with the impacts of a natural hazard event may be one of the most significant drivers of risk perception and demand for insurance (Wachinger et al., 2013[10]; Bronfman et al., 2020[11]; Ren and Wang, 2016[12]; Wang et al., 2012[13]; Gallagher, 2014[14]). For example, one recent survey of consumers in Europe (Belgium, Germany, Romania and Spain) found that the share of households that acquired natural hazard insurance was significantly higher (almost two times higher) among respondents that had had a recent experience with a natural hazard event (64%) relative to those who had not had such an experience (36%) (EIOPA, 2024[4]).

In several emerging and developing Asia and Pacific countries, including Mongolia, Afghanistan, Bangladesh, the Philippines and many of the small island states in the Pacific, a potentially large share of the population has been affected by natural hazards in recent years (Figure 1.8). This is likely to lead to a relatively higher level of risk awareness and perception in Asia than in many other parts of the world where there is more limited experience with natural hazard impacts.

Some insurance companies, intermediaries and/or regulators in Indonesia, Malaysia, Pakistan and Sri Lanka indicated that a lack of risk awareness limits the demand for insurance coverage. In Indonesia, there is some evidence that risk awareness is relatively high, particularly in communities with recent experience (Viverita et al., 2014[15]), although a relatively high level of awareness has not led to the broad implementation of preparedness measures (including the purchase of insurance coverage) (Adhi et al., 2019[16]). In Sri Lanka, there is also some evidence of a high-level of risk perception. For example, a survey by the Disaster Management Centre in Sri Lanka found high levels of awareness and experience with natural hazards among micro, small and medium sized enterprises (MSMEs), while a study that surveyed residents of a highly-exposed community also found high-levels of risk perception among survey respondents (Weerasuriya and Rajapaksha, 2023[17]). In Malaysia, some regions have faced frequent flooding[11] which has likely led to a relatively high-level of flood risk awareness in those areas, although some insurance companies noted that households and businesses outside of those regions often perceive themselves to be at low risk. In Pakistan, despite significant exposure to natural hazard risks and recent experience with major floods,[12] there is some evidence that risk perception is generally low outside of the areas with recent experience (Shah, Rana and Ali, 2023[18]), including urban areas that have faced few major flooding events in recent years. In Pakistan, earthquake risk perception also tends to be lower than flood risk perception as earthquakes have occurred much less frequently. A lack of risk awareness was not identified as a major impediment to the demand for insurance coverage in the Philippines, as natural hazard risk perception is generally considered to be high given the frequency of natural hazard events. For example, one survey across regions and socio-economic groups in the Philippines found that almost half of the respondents perceived there to be a very high or extremely high likelihood that climate change would significantly impact their household within the next five years (Vinck et al., 2024[19]).

Figure 1.8. Estimated share of the population affected by natural hazards annually in recent years

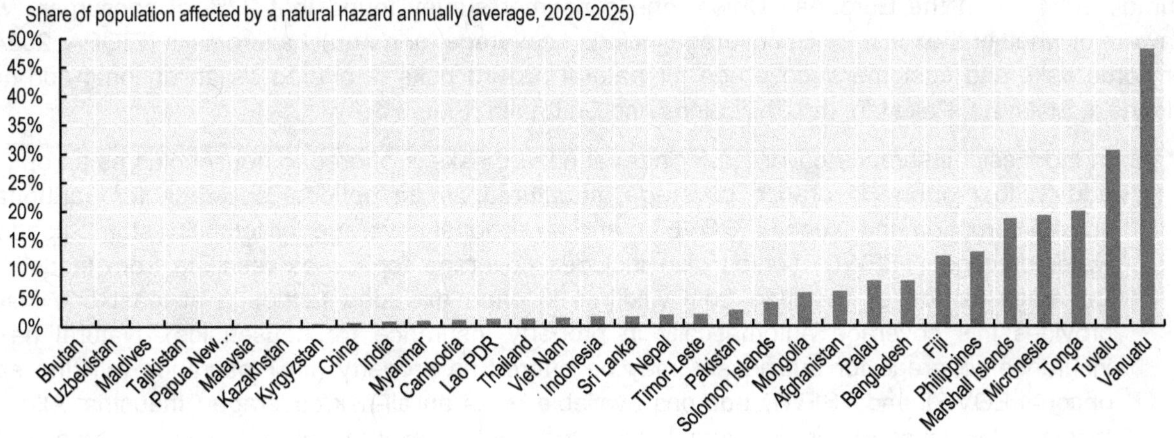

Note: Calculated as the average number of people affected annually by a natural hazard between 2020 and 2025 (Q1) as a share of total population.
Source: OECD calculations based on data on number affected from Centre for Research on the Epidemiology of Disasters (CRED) (n.d.[20]) and population from World Bank (n.d.[21]).

Limited awareness of availability, need for or benefit of insurance coverage for natural hazard risks

A high-level of awareness or perception of exposure to natural hazard risks may not always translate into the implementation of preparedness measures or the acquisition of insurance coverage. Households and businesses may not be aware that coverage for natural hazard risks is available or that they need to acquire specific coverage to protect against damages and losses from natural hazards. They may be unaware of - or may under-value - the benefits of insurance coverage in providing financial protection against these risks, potentially as a result of a lack of trust in insurance companies. A lack of awareness about the need for – and benefits of – financial protection against natural hazard risks was identified by insurance supervisors, intermediaries and/or insurance companies as a driver of protection gaps in Indonesia, Malaysia, Pakistan, the Philippines and Sri Lanka.

A lack of awareness of the availability of insurance coverage for natural hazard risks is unlikely to be a significant factor in limiting demand for insurance coverage in most countries, although it could impact demand among some segments of the population. For example, a survey of European consumers (Belgium, Germany, Romania and Spain) found that 18% of the respondents that had not acquired insurance for natural hazard risks were generally unaware that such coverage exists (EIOPA, 2024[4]). One of the insurance companies in Malaysia that responded to a survey for the development of this report indicated that some segments of the population are unaware of the coverage for natural hazard risks that is available from insurance companies. A survey of residents of the Klang Valley in Malaysia found that 68% would be willing to acquire flood insurance if available (Khairunisa et al., 2023[22]), suggesting that some households may not be aware of the availability of flood insurance coverage (or may not have access, as discussed below).

Households and businesses may be unaware of the need for specific coverage against natural hazard risks if they mistakenly believe that they are covered against these losses through their standard property or fire insurance coverage. This is more likely to occur in countries where coverage for some or all natural hazard losses is only available as an optional addition or endorsement to property insurance coverage ("optional add-on") or as a separate policy ("stand-alone coverage"), rather than as a standard inclusion in property (fire) insurance ("automatic inclusion"). For example, in the United States, where flood insurance is only available as a stand-alone coverage, a recent survey of households found that 56% mistakenly believed that their standard home insurance policy included coverage for flood damages (Insurance Journal, 2024[23]). In the European Union, one consumer survey found that 22% of consumers were unaware of whether their insurance coverage included coverage for natural hazard risks (EIOPA, 2024[4]). For some risks and customers. coverage for natural hazard risks is offered as an optional add-on in Indonesia, Malaysia, Pakistan, the Philippines and Sri Lanka (Figure 1.9):

- In Indonesia, insurance coverage for natural hazard risks is offered to households as an optional add-on to property insurance coverage, structured as an optional coverage for earthquake, volcanic eruption and tsunami (EQVET), and an optional coverage for tempest, storm, flood and water damage (TSFWD) (which also includes coverage for losses resulting from landslides). Coverage for losses resulting from wildfires is often excluded (although at least one insurer provides this coverage automatically in property insurance for households). Natural hazard insurance coverage for businesses may be offered as property (fire) insurance with the same optional EQVET and TSFWD add-ons available or as an all-risk coverage ("Industrial All-Risk") that includes coverage for all natural hazard perils unless explicitly excluded. Insurance coverage for wildfire losses is often included in coverage provided to businesses although approaches differ among insurers.
- In Malaysia, property insurance coverage offered to households tends to take one of two main forms: (i) a standard (or "basic") fire insurance policy where coverage for specific natural hazards can be provided as an optional addition; or (ii) a "houseowner"/"householder" insurance policy that includes coverage for specific natural hazards (hurricane, cyclone, typhoon, windstorm; earthquake and volcanic eruption; and flood). Coverage offered to businesses (particularly SMEs) tends to offer coverage for natural hazard risks as an optional add-on, although a few insurers automatically include coverage for natural hazard risks with an option to opt out of that coverage. There is also an Industrial All-Risk coverage available to businesses which includes coverage for natural hazard risks, unless specifically excluded. Coverage for losses resulting from landslides and wildfires is usually only offered to households and businesses as an optional addition to property insurance coverage.
- In Pakistan, coverage for flood, storm and earthquake losses is automatically included in the property insurance coverage provided to households by some insurers (usually the larger insurers), while smaller insurers may only provide that coverage as an optional add-on. Coverage for landslides, volcanic eruptions and wildfire losses is generally not available, although some insurers offer coverage to households for some or all of these perils, either as an automatic inclusion or optional add-on. For businesses, coverage for flood, storm and earthquake losses may be included automatically or offered as an optional add-on to property insurance coverage, although only a few large insurers offer optional add-on coverage for landslides, volcanic eruptions and wildfire losses, and insurers may choose to not offer coverage for some hazards in high-risk areas.
- In the Philippines, coverage for natural hazard risks is offered to households and businesses as an optional add-on although some insurers indicated that they tend to automatically include coverage for flood, storm and earthquake in the property insurance that they offer. Coverage for losses from landslides and volcanic eruptions is also available as an optional add-on to property insurance policies, although insurers are less likely to include it automatically and may not offer coverage for these hazards in some areas. Insurance coverage for wildfire losses is not generally available (and is also a more limited risk) in the Philippines.

- In Sri Lanka, coverage for natural hazard risks is generally included automatically in the property insurance coverage offered to households and businesses, although the policyholder or insurer may choose not to include coverage for specific perils and practices differ among different insurers. The specific natural hazard perils included in coverage (whether automatically or as an optional add-on) varies across insurers, with some offering bundled coverage (e.g. a "Specific Natural Perils Cover" that typically covers flood, storm and earthquake losses) and others providing coverage for named perils (which may include flood, storm, earthquake as well as tsunami and volcanic eruption). Coverage for landslide and wildfire losses is generally not available to businesses or households.

Figure 1.9. Approaches to offering natural hazard insurance coverage to households and businesses

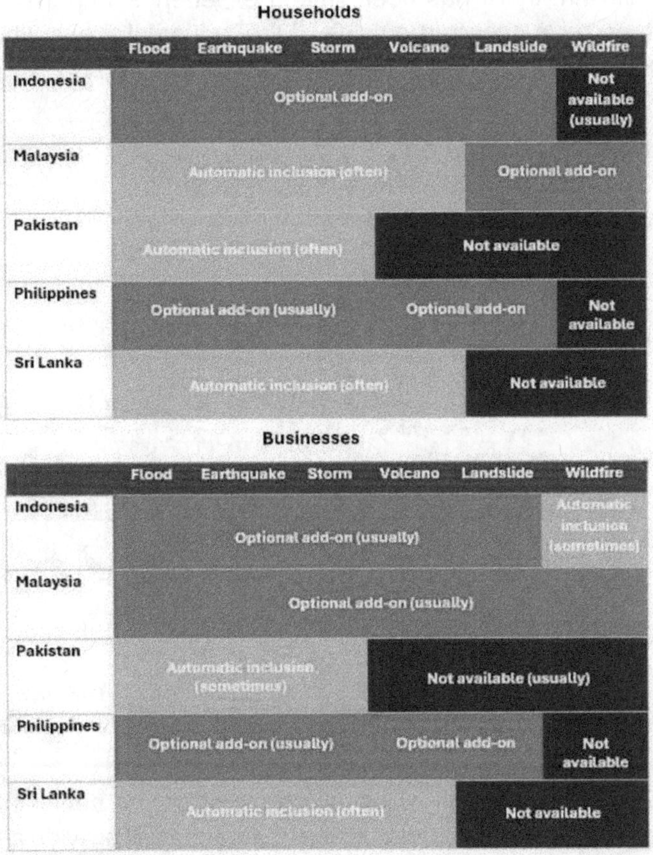

Awareness of the need for coverage against natural hazard risks may also be lower if households and businesses expect that the government will take on responsibility for recovery and reconstruction and provide financial assistance or compensation to those affected by natural hazards. This is often cited as a concern in OECD countries and there is some evidence that consumers decide not to acquire insurance because they expect to be compensated by governments for any damages due to natural hazards. For example, surveys undertaken in a number of European countries found that between 4% and 15% of uninsured households[13] did not acquire insurance because of an expectation that the government will provide compensation (EIOPA, 2024[4]). This concern was raised among some insurance supervisors, intermediaries and/or insurance companies in Indonesia, Malaysia, Pakistan, the Philippines and Sri Lanka, although it was generally limited to vulnerable segments of society (e.g. rural or low-income households) that are more likely to receive government assistance and less likely to acquire insurance coverage even without an expectation of government assistance.

Awareness of the availability and need for insurance coverage against natural hazard risks may be insufficient to achieve broad levels of coverage if households and businesses have limited awareness of the benefits of insurance coverage for providing financial protection. Awareness of the benefits of insurance is likely to be higher where households and businesses have previous experience with insurance. For example, positive previous experience with insurance, whether for natural hazard losses or other types of losses or expenses, is likely to increase the tendency of a household or business to consider insurance as a means to protect against natural hazard risks (EIOPA, 2024[4]).

Households and businesses in countries with lower levels of insurance penetration will have less previous experience with insurance. The non-life insurance penetration rate in most countries in emerging and developing Asia and Pacific, including in Indonesia, Malaysia, Pakistan, the Philippines and Sri Lanka, is less than half of the average penetration rate in OECD countries (Figure 1.10). Specific experience with insurance coverage for natural hazard risks is likely to also be low where there are significant protection gaps. For example, in Pakistan, there has been limited experience with insured natural hazard losses, particularly as recent losses have occurred outside of the industrial areas where insurance coverage is more likely to have been acquired.

Figure 1.10. Non-life insurance penetration

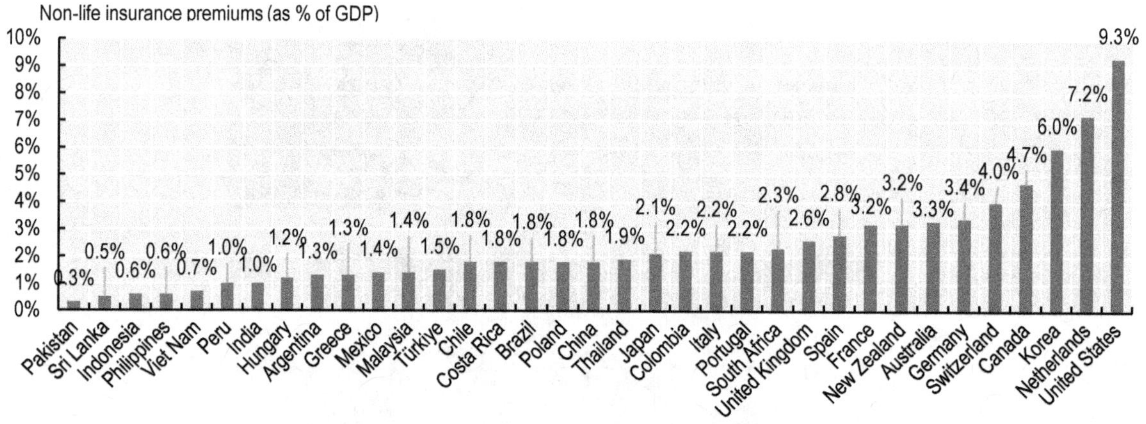

Source: Swiss Re Institute (2024[24]), World insurance: strengthening global resilience with a new lease of life, https://www.swissre.com/institute/research/sigma-research/sigma-2024-03-world-insurance-global-resilience.html.

An understanding of the potential benefits of insurance might not be sufficient to encourage take-up of coverage if households and businesses do not trust that insurance will provide an effective form of financial protection at a fair price. For example, a survey of consumers in a number of European countries (France, Greece, Italy and Spain) found that 7.4% to 13.1% of respondents without insurance did not acquire insurance because they do not trust that insurance companies will pay, while a further 9.0% to 11.3% remained uninsured because they do not trust insurance companies to offer fair prices (EIOPA, 2024[4]). In Indonesia, a national survey used for the development of the National Strategy on Indonesian Financial Literacy found that while 62% of respondents understood the benefits of insurance, only 10% of respondents had confidence in the insurance sector (OJK, 2021[25]). A lack of trust in insurance companies' capacity or willingness to pay claims for natural hazard-related losses in a timely manner was raised by public and private sector stakeholders in Sri Lanka. Insurance companies indicated that misconceptions about coverage, policy terms and claims processes contributed to low levels of trust in insurance. However, a survey by the Insurance Regulatory Commission of Sri Lanka published in 2024 found that 49% of respondents were confident or extremely confident in the general insurance sector (IRCSL and University of Colombo, 2024[26]).

Factors such as gender, age, education, insurance literacy and, particularly, experience with insurance affect trust in insurance (Courbage and Nicolas, 2019[27]). Cultural factors such as religion can also have an impact. For example, some studies have found a higher level of trust in sharia-compliant and takaful insurance coverage in countries with significant Muslim populations (Hassan and Abbas, 2019[28]; Souiden and Jabeur, 2015[29]).

Limited capacity or willingness to pay for natural hazard insurance coverage

Even where there is high awareness of natural hazard risks and an understanding of the availability and benefit of specific insurance coverage for these risks, limited income and competing spending demands may limit the ability of households and businesses to afford insurance coverage. The cost of insurance was identified by insurance supervisors, intermediaries and/or insurance companies as a driver of protection gaps in Indonesia, Malaysia, Pakistan, the Philippines and Sri Lanka, particularly for low-income households and SMEs. There is some evidence that low-income households are less likely to acquire insurance coverage. For example, in Europe, households with less than EUR 30 000 in annual income were found to be less likely to purchase home insurance than households with higher income (EIOPA, 2024[4]). In one survey of urban residents in Indonesia that had experienced climate-related extreme events, a lack of resources was among the most common reasons for not taking preparedness measures, such as acquiring insurance (Adhi et al., 2019[16]).

The premiums that insurance companies charge for natural hazard insurance coverage depends on: (i) their assessment of risk (i.e. the probability of incurring losses that would be covered by the policy); (ii) distribution and operating expenses (including commissions, underwriting and loss adjustment expenses as well as the cost of reinsurance); and (iii) market and competitive considerations. Lower risk, lower distribution and operating expenses, and more competitive markets can support affordability and reduce insurance costs.

In most countries, insurance supervisors also impose some requirements on insurers that are applicable when establishing premiums for the coverage that they provide. In some countries, supervisors take a principles-based approach that requires insurance companies to charge premiums that are adequate and not unfairly discriminatory – which may be subject to supervisory review either as a condition for approval or at the discretion of the supervisor. In other countries, supervisors impose quantitative requirements, such as a fixed premium (usually based on sum insured), a minimum or maximum premium, or a range of acceptable premium rates. Box 1.1 provides an overview of supervisory requirements and market approaches to premium setting in Indonesia, Malaysia, Pakistan, the Philippines and Sri Lanka.

Box 1.1. Pricing approaches and supervisory oversight in Indonesia, Malaysia, Pakistan, the Philippines and Sri Lanka

The insurance supervisors in Indonesia, the Philippines and Sri Lanka require insurers to submit new insurance products providing coverage for natural hazard risks for prior approval. In Malaysia, prior approval is only required for products with premium rates that deviate by more than 30% from the Revised Fire Tariff (see below). In Pakistan, there are no prior approval requirements for insurance products that provide coverage for natural hazard risks.

In Indonesia and the Philippines, insurance coverage for natural hazard risks is subject to pricing guidance or references. In Indonesia, pricing for property and natural hazard insurance coverage is based on occupancy and construction characteristics (for fire), hazard zone (for EQVET and TSFWD) and number of floors (for EQVET) – although insurance companies can deviate from the pricing guidance. In the Philippines, a minimum premium rate is required for property (fire) and natural hazard (typhoon, flood and earthquake) insurance coverage and insurers are required to set premiums at or above the minimum rate (subject to fines for non-compliance). Due to market dynamics (competitive pressure) and risk assessment challenges (see below), the minimum rates are very often applied as fixed rates by insurers in Indonesia and the Philippines. Insurers in Indonesia and the Philippines do not generally charge higher premiums in higher risk areas, although some Indonesian insurers impose higher deductibles in high-risk areas (which is not permitted in the Philippines).

In Malaysia, as part of a broader initiative to eliminate fixed (tariff) pricing, pricing consistent with the Revised Fire Tariff must be offered although insurers can also offer products that are not subject to those rates (i.e. non-tariff products). As noted above, without prior approval, pricing of non-tariff products cannot be more than 30% lower than the pricing of the tariff products. Many insurers tend to price coverage for natural hazard risks in both tariff and non-tariff products at the fixed rate of sum insured defined for tariff products, although insurers do have the flexibility to price natural hazard coverage at rates that are 30% above or below the fixed tariff rate (without prior approval). Some insurers have been introducing higher rates and (particularly) higher deductibles for flood insurance coverage in high-risk areas.

In Pakistan and Sri Lanka, insurers are free to choose the premium rates that they apply for property and natural hazard insurance coverage, although pricing approaches may be subject to supervisory review in Sri Lanka as part of product approval. In Sri Lanka, some insurers charge higher premiums in high-risk areas (and lower premiums in low-risk areas) although higher deductibles (or sub-limits and exclusions) appear to be more commonly applied to address higher levels of risk. In Pakistan, higher deductibles are often required for property insurance coverage that includes coverage for natural hazard risks. Insurers in Pakistan also vary premium pricing based on risk characteristics, particularly for commercial clients.

Households and small businesses with limited income or revenue may not be able to afford the cost of insurance coverage given other spending demands while, where premiums vary with risk, those located in high-risk areas or in poorly constructed buildings may face high premium costs beyond their capacity to pay.

The cost of coverage including coverage for natural hazard risks appears unlikely to create "affordability stress" for most households.[14] This is based on a limited review of online offers of household property insurance coverage in Indonesia, Malaysia, Pakistan and the Philippines.[15] Average household property insurance premiums would appear to cost less than two weeks of average household (gross) income in all four countries (and less than one week in the case of Malaysia). However, the estimated average household insurance premium could cost slightly more than four weeks of average household income for the 20% lowest income households in the Philippines and just under four weeks of the minimum wage income in Indonesia for homes with lower constructions standards (Figure 1.11, left-side), although this would likely be offset by lower property values that would result in lower premiums.

However, an "affordable" premium may not be sufficient to incentivise purchase where property insurance coverage or natural hazard insurance coverage is voluntary. Households or businesses may not be willing to pay for coverage even if that coverage is affordable, which may be driven by the factors related to perceptions of exposure to natural hazard risk or the benefits of acquiring specific insurance coverage for those risks. In one of the surveys of European consumers, uninsured households in France, Greece, Italy and Spain provided an indication of the amount that they would be willing to pay for household insurance coverage (including natural hazard insurance coverage). While the amount varied across the four countries, an overall preference equivalent to approximately 0.95% of gross income appeared to be broadly acceptable (EIOPA, 2024[4]). The estimated average premium cost, for the average home in Indonesia, Malaysia, Pakistan and the Philippines, would be significantly higher than 0.95% of income in most cases, and up to 7 or 8 times this amount among low-income and high-risk households in Indonesia and low-income households in the Philippines (Figure 1.11, right-side).

Figure 1.11. Illustrations of the cost of insurance relative to affordability and willingness-to-pay

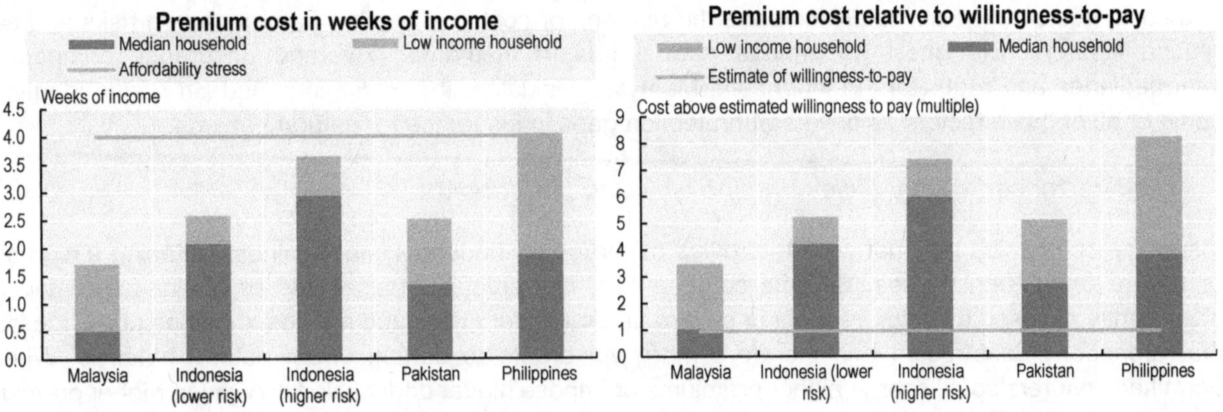

Note: The estimates of premiums costs were calculated based on online premium calculators and premium guidance in all four countries. The following rates per 1 000 in coverage (2.28 (Indonesia, low risk), 3.22 (Indonesia, high risk), 2.66 (Malaysia), 1.83 (Pakistan) and 2.98 (Philippines)) were applied to the following house values: IDR 800 million (Indonesia), MYR 370 000 (Malaysia), PKR 11.5 million (Pakistan) and PHP 4.25 million (Philippines). Data on income distribution for Malaysia (Department of Statistics Malaysia, 2022[30]), Pakistan (Pakistan Bureau of Statistics, 2020[31]) and the Philippines (Philippines Statistics Authority, 2023[32]) and data on basic and median salaries in Indonesia (reported in (Mulya, 2023[33])) were used to calculate weekly income and willingness-to-pay (by applying an estimate of willingness-to-pay for coverage of 0.95% of income, derived from (EIOPA, 2024[4])). Estimates of premium costs were not available for Sri Lanka.

Given significant exposure to natural hazards, the cost of natural hazard coverage often accounts for a significant share of the premium costs for household and business property insurance coverage in many Asian countries. For example, under the Revised Fire Tariff in Malaysia, coverage against natural hazards (particularly floods) accounts for approximately 30-60% of the cost of household property insurance depending on the type of construction. In the Philippines, the minimum premiums for earthquake, typhoon and flood coverage account for 60% of the cost of premiums for homes. In Indonesia, the cost of TSFWD and (particularly) EQVET coverage accounts for 60-70% of the cost of property insurance for households in low-risk earthquake zones and more than 80% of premium cost in high-risk zones (for homes with steel or wood construction).

Where coverage for natural hazard risks is an optional add-on, the significant additional cost of this coverage could be an impediment to purchasing this coverage among price-sensitive and lower-income consumers. The additional cost of optional natural hazard coverage was identified as a driver of protection gaps by some insurers in Malaysia, where approximately 50% of households with property insurance choose to acquire the optional coverage for natural hazard risks. This was also identified as a driver of protection gaps in Indonesia where only a small share of households that acquire property insurance choose to acquire the optional coverage for natural hazard risks. For example, one Indonesian insurance company indicated that less than 5% of its household customers had acquired the optional coverage for flood risk.

1.2.2. Factors that limit the willingness of insurance companies to provide natural hazard insurance coverage – supply factors

Given the potential for catastrophic losses, assuming natural hazard risks can create challenges for insurance companies. Natural hazard risks can impact large areas and many households and businesses simultaneously. The potential for large and correlated losses reduces the benefits of diversification upon which the insurance business model is based and requires insurance companies to set aside significant reserves and acquire substantial reinsurance coverage to ensure that they have sufficient resources to respond to those losses. The relatively low frequency of natural hazards and the complexity in assessing potential impacts leads to greater uncertainty about the potential losses that might be incurred. Higher levels of exposure or vulnerability to natural hazard risks, more limited data and tools for risk assessment and costly reinsurance ultimately increase the risk and/or cost in assuming natural hazard risks and can reduce insurers' willingness to provide natural hazard insurance coverage. Insurance companies, intermediaries and regulators in Indonesia, Malaysia, Pakistan, the Philippines and Sri Lanka identified some or all of these factors as drivers of protection gaps in insurance for natural hazards.

Highly exposed communities, businesses and households

Insurance companies may not want to provide coverage for households or businesses facing a high risk of severe or frequent losses. Specific communities, or particular households or businesses, may be significantly exposed to either frequent or severe natural hazard risks and may have homes or businesses that are poorly constructed and therefore more vulnerable to damage from natural hazards. Where permitted, insurers could charge higher premiums or impose higher deductibles. However, higher premium rates may be unaffordable or unattractive in highly competitive markets while higher deductibles could have reputational impacts if natural hazard losses are rarely reimbursed because they fall below the policyholder deductible. Insurance supervisors and some intermediaries and insurance companies in Indonesia, Malaysia, Pakistan, the Philippines and Sri Lanka indicated that the availability of affordable coverage in high-risk areas is a driver of protection gaps.

Some insurance supervisors impose limitations on the premium rates that insurance companies can apply to the insurance coverage of natural hazard risks that they offer to households and businesses (Box 1.1). This includes guidance on minimum and maximum premium rates in Indonesia, a requirement for prior approval of premium rates that deviate substantially below the tariff rate in Malaysia and minimum premium rates in the Philippines. While insurers are authorised to set premium rates for higher-risk businesses and households at higher rates, highly competitive insurance markets have, in general, led insurers to apply minimum (or tariff) rates to all policyholders and make limited use of the flexibility to charge higher rates, particularly in Indonesia and the Philippines (although as noted above, some insurers in Indonesia and Malaysia will impose higher deductibles or limit the sum insured for specific hazards when offering coverage to higher-risk households and businesses).

As a result of this competitive dynamic, insurers may not offer any coverage for natural hazard risks or specific natural hazard risks in areas where the prevailing market rates are likely to be inadequate to cover probable claims payments:

- In Indonesia, insurers may not offer coverage in areas exposed to annual (or regular) river or coastal flooding or in communities in the highest earthquake risk zone or with recent flood or earthquake claims experience. This is likely also a reflection of weaknesses in risk management which hinder the ability of insurance companies to offer affordable coverage.
- In Malaysia, some insurers do not offer coverage for flood or landslides in areas known to be at high risk. One recent survey of business in Malaysia, for example, found that 17% of SMEs with recent flood experience (within three years) were unable to receive a quote for flood insurance coverage (World Bank and Bank Negara Malaysia, 2024[34]).
- In the Philippines, households and businesses may have difficulty accessing insurance coverage in communities near active fault lines or subject to frequent ground-shaking, communities near active volcanoes and in areas exposed to flood or typhoon risks. For example, one insurance website reviewed for this report clearly stated that flood-prone areas could not be insured against flood and typhoon risks.

Flexibility in setting premiums, deductibles and insured limits does not necessarily ensure coverage availability in markets with price-sensitive consumers. Insurers in Pakistan and Sri Lanka are free to charge higher premiums, impose higher deductibles and limit the sum insured for specific hazards in high-risk areas. In Sri Lanka, insurance companies consider a broad range of criteria for determining which areas might be at high risk that capture communities in coastal regions exposed to coastal flooding and tsunamis, valleys and low-lying areas exposed to flooding, and mountainous regions exposed to earthquakes and landslides. In Pakistan, premium pricing that reflects higher risk is more often applied in property insurance for businesses. However, in both countries, insurers can and do decline coverage for specific hazard risks to households and businesses located in risk-prone areas.

Weaknesses in land-use and development planning, deficient or poorly enforced building codes and insufficient investment in risk reduction and adaptation will clearly have an impact on the pervasiveness of high-risk communities, households and businesses.[16] Insurance companies, intermediaries and regulators in Indonesia, Malaysia, Pakistan, the Philippines and Sri Lanka emphasised the criticality of improving risk management, risk reduction and adaptation for addressing protection gaps in natural hazard insurance.

Difficulties in understanding or quantifying natural hazard risk

Insurance companies may be unwilling to provide coverage for natural hazard risks if they face challenges in understanding or quantifying the potential frequency and severity of losses under any coverage provided. Given the relatively low frequency of natural hazards compared to other types of insured risk, such as motor vehicle accidents, natural hazard risks are difficult to quantify using traditional statistical and actuarial methods. The uncertainty of loss frequency and the potential for severe losses may discourage insurers from providing coverage for these risks. The changing frequency and severity of many weather-related risks exacerbates this uncertainty.

The insurance sector uses a number of approaches to assessing natural hazard risk to support underwriting and pricing decisions. These include their own past claims data and loss experience, hazard or risk maps and zones provided by local or national governments or other organisations, risk ratings developed by local or international intermediaries and reinsurance companies, and catastrophe models developed internally or provided by intermediaries, reinsurers or specialised catastrophe modelling companies. These approaches vary in terms of their accuracy and availability:

- Catastrophe models, which are developed using real and simulated natural hazard events and data on buildings and structural vulnerabilities, provide the most sophisticated approach to assessing natural hazard risks and can (to some extent) be calibrated to take into account climate change through "climate-conditioning."[17] However, models are not always available for assessing risks in emerging and developing markets and coverage for some types of natural hazards risks is much more limited (Figure 1.12). They can also be costly to acquire, particularly for smaller insurers.
- Hazard maps and risk zones vary in terms of quality. In some countries, developed and emerging, insurance companies have limited trust in the accuracy of the hazard and risk maps developed by governments.
- The value of past claims data for assessing risk and underwriting coverage is generally more limited for infrequent events such as natural hazard risks. Relying on claims data will also pose particular challenges in countries where insurance coverage of natural hazard risks is limited (thereby limiting the number of claims) and where climate change is having significant impacts on the frequency and/or severity of weather-related hazards.

Figure 1.12. Catastrophe model coverage in Asia-Pacific

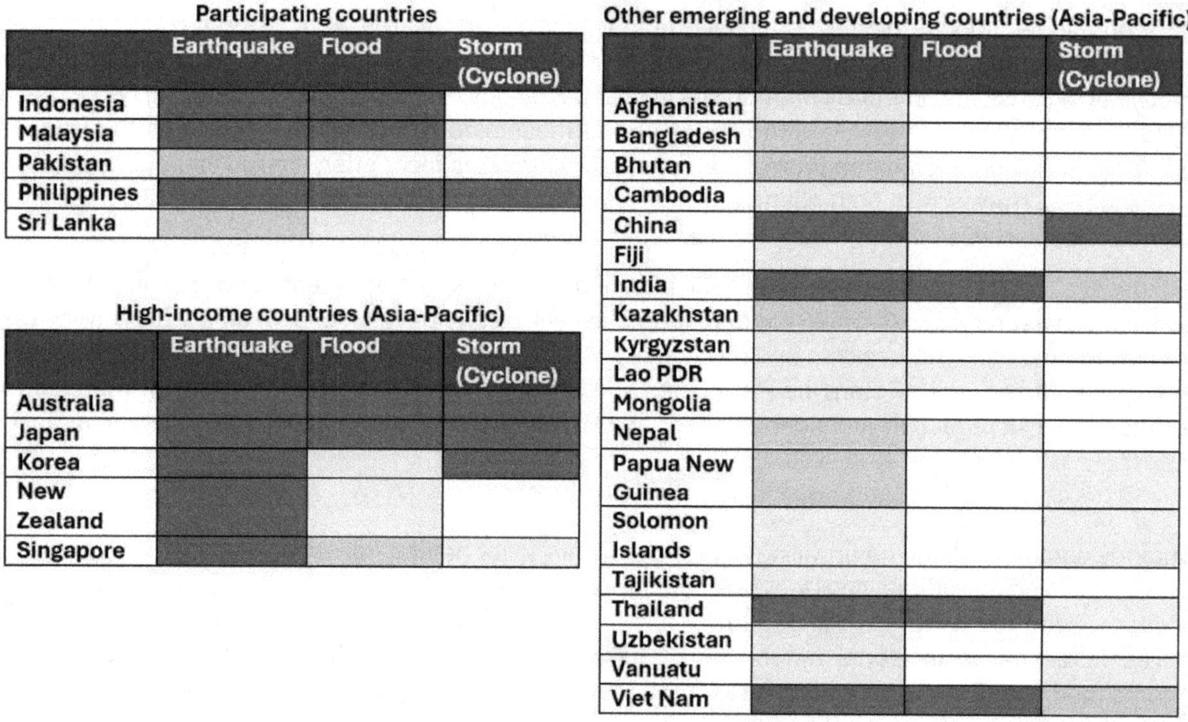

Note: Dark blue shading indicates that three or more models are available. Medium blue shading indicates that two models are available. Light blue shading indicates that one model is available.

Source: OECD based on data on model availability from Aon (2024[35]), Moody's (2025[36]), (2025[37]), (2025[38]), (2025[39]), Verisk Analytics (2025[40]), CATRisk Solutions (n.d.[41]), Risk Frontiers (n.d.[42]), COMBUS (n.d.[43]), Insurance Development Forum (2025[44]).

The development of these different risk assessment tools – and their ultimate accuracy – depends on the availability and quality of data that is normally provided by governments, including hazard maps, data on past hazard events and their impacts, as well as data on exposure (i.e. building stock). Incomplete, inaccessible or low-quality data from governments will limit the accuracy of – and confidence in – risk assessment tools that are developed based on this data. A lack of comprehensive and updated data on property valuations and/or building inventories was identified as challenges in Pakistan and the Philippines. In Malaysia, one recent analysis identified limited scope and granularity, a short historical record and access restrictions as limitations in the flood risk data available to financial institutions (World Bank and Bank Negara Malaysia, 2024[34]). Some insurance companies highlighted efforts (since discontinued) to access more granular data from governments on past inundation levels. In Sri Lanka, limited trust in the accuracy of government-provided flood maps was identified by some insurers as an impediment to their use in underwriting coverage.

Figure 1.13 provides an overview of the main approaches taken by insurers to assessing natural hazard risks in Indonesia, Malaysia, Pakistan, the Philippines and Sri Lanka. In the Philippines, while some insurers have access to catastrophe modelling tools for earthquake, flood and storm/cyclone risks, insurance companies generally rely on hazard maps and past claims data as the primary basis for underwriting coverage. Similarly, in Indonesia and Malaysia, different insurers use different risk assessment tools. In Indonesia, risk ratings are most commonly used as a basis for underwriting flood, storm and volcano risks, and risk zones are most commonly applied for earthquake risks although insurers also have access to models for flood, earthquake and volcano risks, including from Maipark, a local reinsurer for earthquake risk. Similarly, in Malaysia, some insurers use models, risk ratings and hazard maps for underwriting earthquake, flood and storm risks, although past claims data appear to be the main basis for underwriting coverage among most insurers, including aggregate industry-wide data provided by Insurance Services Malaysia (ISM). In Pakistan and Sri Lanka, past claims and loss data are used as the main basis for underwriting coverage for all natural hazard risks although insurers in Pakistan also access mapping tools made available by international reinsurers and intermediaries. Limited past insured losses and the low quality of some insurers' claims data, as well as changes in hazard frequency and severity, were identified as challenges to the use of past loss data for underwriting coverage, either by insurance companies or regulators (or both) in Sri Lanka and Pakistan as well as in Malaysia and the Philippines.

Figure 1.13. Primary basis for underwriting natural hazard insurance

<table>
<tr><th></th><th>Earthquake</th><th>Flood</th><th>Storm</th><th>Volcano</th><th>Landslide</th><th>Wildfire</th></tr>
<tr><td>Indonesia</td><td>Hazard maps and past claims</td><td colspan="2">Risk ratings and past claims</td><td>Hazard maps and past claims</td><td colspan="2">Past claims</td></tr>
<tr><td>Malaysia</td><td colspan="2">Hazard maps and past claims</td><td>Risk ratings and past claims</td><td colspan="3">Past claims</td></tr>
<tr><td>Pakistan</td><td colspan="6">Past claims</td></tr>
<tr><td>Philippines</td><td colspan="6">Hazard maps and past claims</td></tr>
<tr><td>Sri Lanka</td><td colspan="6">Past claims</td></tr>
</table>

Note: As noted above, insurance companies use various risk assessment tools for the different types of hazards. The figure illustrates what appears to be the most common tool used by insurers.
Source: Prepared based on responses to a survey circulated to insurance regulators and insurance companies and discussions with regulatory and insurance market representatives.

There is some evidence that the challenges related to risk assessment, whether due to a lack of data or a lack of risk assessment tools, have had an impact on insurance companies. In Sri Lanka, one public sector agency indicated that a lack of data made insurance companies reluctant to provide coverage for natural hazard risks. Insurance companies in Sri Lanka indicated that a lack of risk assessment tools has led to conservative underwriting, higher deductibles and coverage exclusions. In Malaysia, one analysis found that the inability to accurately assess risks exposures and quantify potential losses has limited insurance companies' use of risk-based pricing (World Bank and Bank Negara Malaysia, 2024[34]). As discussed in the next section, there have also been impacts on reinsurance access and pricing for some insurers in some countries.

Limited access to affordable reinsurance coverage

Due to the potential for severe and correlated losses, insurance companies that assume natural hazard risks will usually transfer some portion of that risk to reinsurance markets. Global reinsurance and capital markets play a critical role in providing additional financial capacity to absorb natural hazard losses and diversify natural hazard risk internationally (OECD, 2018[45]).

Reinsurers provide two main types of reinsurance coverage: (i) proportional coverage (i.e. where premiums and claims are shared on a proportional basis); and (ii) non-proportional coverage (i.e. where reinsurance coverage is provided for losses above a certain threshold). Both types of reinsurance coverage are accessed to protect against property and natural hazard risks, although non-proportional reinsurance is inherently designed to protect against the severe losses that could result from catastrophes such as natural hazard events. Reinsurance can be provided on a facultative basis (i.e. as a reinsurance coverage for a specific, usually large, policyholder) or treaty basis (i.e. as a reinsurance coverage for a portfolio of policyholders).

Insurers have also increasingly transferred risk to capital markets through insurance-linked securities (e.g. catastrophe bonds[18]) and other alternative reinsurance structures such as collateralised reinsurance, sidecars and industry loss warranties.[19] However, traditional reinsurance remains the main source of coverage for most insurers. Capital backing traditional reinsurance accounted for approximately 82% of all reinsurance capital in 2024 (Guy Carpenter, 2025[46]).

In most countries, insurers cede a significant share of the property insurance premiums that they collect to reinsurance markets. Emerging and developing market insurers tend to cede more to reinsurers than insurers in high-income countries (65%, on average, relative to 34% in high-income countries). Insurers in Indonesia, Pakistan, the Philippines and Sri Lanka cede more to reinsurers than the simple average for emerging and developing markets (Figure 1.14).

Figure 1.14. Share of property insurance premiums ceded to reinsurers (cession ratio)

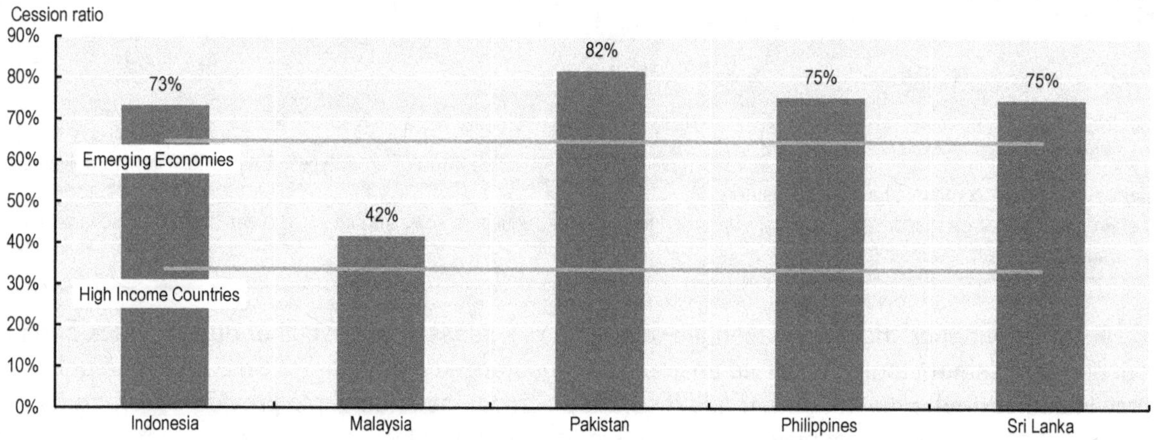

Note: Calculated as the simple average of premiums ceded as a share of gross written premium for the "Fire and other property insurance" class of insurance for all reporting countries and available years between 2012 and 2023 from the OECD Data Explorer. For Pakistan, data is from SECP reports on Insurance Industry Statistics (2021-23 data years). For the Philippines, data is from the Insurance Commission's Annual Reports (2013-22 data years). For Sri Lanka, data is from IRCSL Statistical Reviews (2015-23 data years). Countries are classified as high-income based on the World Bank Country and Lending Groups (World Bank, 2025[47])
Source: OECD based on data in premiums written and ceded from OECD (2025[48]), Insurance Commission (2015[49]), (2017[50]), (2019[51]), (2021[52]), (2023[53]), SECP (2022[54]), (2024[55]), IRCSL (2018[56]), (2020[57]), (2022[58]), (2024[59]).

The cost and availability of reinsurance tends to be cyclical. Large reinsurance industry losses tend to lead to an increase in pricing and decrease in availability, referred to as a "hard market", which tends to stabilise over time as new capacity enters the market and competition leads to lower pricing (OECD, 2018[45]).

Figure 1.15 provides an overview of reinsurance pricing trends for property catastrophe risks, based on the Guy Carpenter Global and APAC (Asia-Pacific) Property Catastrophe Rate on Line indices. The Global index shows significant pricing increases after large hurricane losses in the United States in 2005. The APAC index shows significant increases after major flooding in Thailand and a major earthquake in Japan in 2011. Both the Global and APAC indices indicate hard market conditions in recent years with pricing that was 2-25% higher in 2023 and 2024 than in 2004. In the recent hard market, higher attachment points have also been applied which has required primary insurers to retain more of the risk and ultimate claims. For example, prior to 2023, an estimated 20% of global "catastrophe losses" were absorbed by reinsurers – although this declined to an estimated 14% in 2024 (Guy Carpenter, 2024[60]).

Figure 1.15. Reinsurance pricing (Guy Carpenter Property Catastrophe Rate on Line Index)

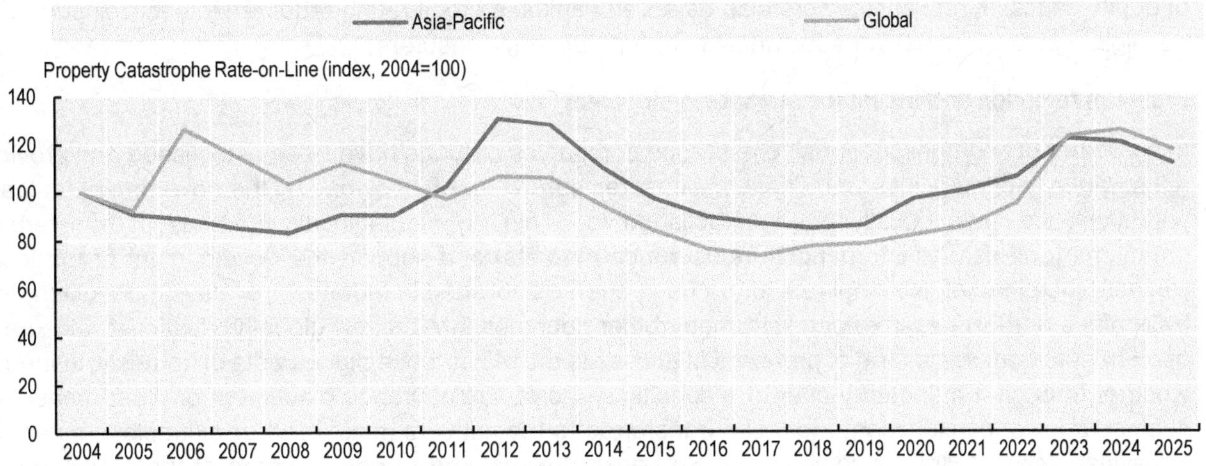

Note: The Guy Carpenter Global Property Catastrophe Rate on Line Index provides data from 1990 although the Guy Carpenter APAC Property Catastrophe Rate on Line Index only provides data from 2004. To provide a comparison on pricing trends, the global index was adjusted to make 2004 the base year. The indices are calculated based on the change in the USD cost of coverage for excess-of-loss reinsurance placements by brokers for a consistent reinsurance programme.
Source: OECD calculations based on Guy Carpenter (2024[61]), (2024[62]) (using individual figures published in Artemis (2025[63]) and (2025[64])).

In addition to global and regional reinsurance pricing trends, a number of factors specific to national insurance markets and individual insurers also have important impacts on cost and access to reinsurance coverage, including loss experience, data quality and, particularly in the case of proportional reinsurance, pricing adequacy.[20] The policy and regulatory framework (Box 1.2) can also have impacts on access to affordable reinsurance. Limited access to reinsurance, higher pricing and/or higher attachment points can limit direct insurer appetite and can have a significant impact on the availability and affordability of property insurance for households and businesses – particularly for insurers and insurance markets that rely heavily on transferring risks to reinsurance markets.

Box 1.2. Policy and regulatory requirements related to risk transfer to reinsurance markets

Mitigating risk to primary insurers

The transfer of risk to reinsurance markets creates risks for the ceding insurer, including counterparty risks (the risk that the reinsurer will not pay valid claims) and execution risks (the risk that reinsurance coverage does not respond as expected by the cedant). Insurance regulators and supervisors oversee and impose requirements on primary insurers' use of reinsurance to mitigate these risks, including by requiring insurers to submit their annual reinsurance plans and ensuring that insurers implement risk retention and transfer approaches consistent with their financial capacity. For example, in Indonesia, insurers are required to meet quantitative requirements on minimum and maximum retention as a share of equity capital. Many supervisors also establish minimum credit rating requirements for reinsurers to be eligible to assume risk (or substantial risk) from domestic insurers.[1]

Premium retention and insurance market development

In a number of countries, national reinsurance companies or funds have been established and provide reinsurance to primary insurers. These national reinsurers are often owned by the government (at least partially)[2] and have usually been established to retain premiums locally (instead of transferring premiums (and risk) to international reinsurance markets) and support the development of the local (re)insurance market. National reinsurers have been established in Indonesia, Malaysia, Pakistan, the Philippines and Sri Lanka (along with many other countries in Asia and globally). National reinsurers often benefit from some form of preferential access to the reinsurance placements of domestic insurers, whether through a mandatory offer of a specific share of a reinsurance placement or other measures such as a lower capital charge for risks transferred to the national reinsurer. For example, insurers in Malaysia, Pakistan, the Philippines and Sri Lanka are required to offer a share of their reinsurance placements to the national reinsurer.[3] In Malaysia, insurers are also required to maximise local retention while the placements with the national reinsurers in Malaysia and Sri Lanka (as well as other "resident" reinsurers in Malaysia) benefit from a lower capital charge than placements with other reinsurers. In Indonesia, a former system of preferential placements with domestic reinsurers (government-owned and private sector reinsurers) was loosened in 2020 for "non-simple" risks including property-related risks, allowing insurers to transfer risk to reinsurers based in jurisdictions with a bilateral agreement with Indonesia. As discussed below, the national reinsurers play different roles in the markets of each country and therefore have different impacts on the availability and affordability of reinsurance coverage.

Notes:

1. For example, in Pakistan, 80% of ceded risk must be placed with reinsurers rated A (S&P) or above and no risk can be placed with a foreign reinsurer with a rating below BBB (S&P). In Sri Lanka, insurers can only transfer risk to reinsurers with a rating of B+ (A.M. Best) or above. In the Philippines, foreign reinsurers must be represented by a resident agent to be eligible to assume risk which requires that the foreign reinsurer has capital levels equivalent to what is required of domestic counterparts in the Philippines and a minimum credit rating (A- (A.M. Best), Aa (Moody's), AA (Fitch, S&P)).

2. For example, in Sri Lanka, the national reinsurance company (National Insurance Trust Fund) is wholly-owned by the government. In Pakistan, the national reinsurer (Pakistan Reinsurance Corporation) is partially listed although the government is the major shareholder. In Malaysia and the Philippines, a government-owned agency or fund has a major shareholding in the national reinsurer (Malaysia Re and Nat Re in the Philippines). In Indonesia, there are two reinsurers that are wholly-owned by the government (Indonesia Re and Nasional Re) and a few private sector domestic reinsurers, including a reinsurer established by the insurance sector to assume earthquake risk (Maipark).

3. In Malaysia, 2.5% of all proportional treaty placements must be offered to Malaysia Re. In Pakistan, 35% of all treaty reinsurance placements must be offered to the Pakistan Reinsurance Corporation and all facultative placements must be offered to domestic insurers. In the Philippines, Nat Re must be offered 10% of all outward reinsurance placements, and facultative placements must be offered to at least two domestic insurers. In Sri Lanka, 30% of each treaty and facultative reinsurance placement must be offered to the National Insurance Trust Fund.

Some insurance supervisors, intermediaries and/or insurance companies in Indonesia, Malaysia, Pakistan, the Philippines and Sri Lanka identified challenges related to the cost and availability of reinsurance as a driver of protection gaps – although with some differences in terms of impact:

- In Malaysia, changes in reinsurance appetite have been generally consistent with changes in the broader reinsurance market although the large floods that affected urban areas in 2021-22 have led reinsurers to impose tighter conditions and higher retentions. The reinsurance market is reportedly satisfied with pricing in Malaysia, including the generally applied tariff rate for flood coverage, which has helped maintain the availability of proportional reinsurance capacity. Most insurers transfer risk to reinsurers on a proportional basis although there are also some limited non-proportional treaty arrangements.
- In the Philippines, insurance companies have been impacted by the increase in pricing as a result of the hard market, although capacity has reportedly remained available for most insurers. Concerns about the adequacy of the minimum pricing as well as a lack of adherence to the minimum pricing requirement by some insurers has led to a reduction in proportional reinsurance capacity and a shift towards non-proportional excess-of-loss coverage with higher retention requirements imposed. The non-proportional coverage has been costly although the higher retentions have reportedly incentivised improved pricing discipline among insurers.
- In Pakistan, there has been a reduction in the number of international reinsurers willing to offer coverage (and act as lead reinsurers) and some concerns about data quality. However, larger insurers have been able to maintain their access to international reinsurance markets, driven in part by a perception that pricing is adequate. Some smaller insurers, who generally acquire proportional reinsurance coverage, have faced some constraints on access to reinsurance coverage. These challenges led the insurance regulator (the Securities and Exchange Commission of Pakistan) to temporarily relax the requirements on foreign reinsurer ratings in order to relieve some of the challenges in accessing capacity.
- In Indonesia, access to affordable reinsurance has been more challenging. Past preferential placements with domestic reinsurers led to international reinsurer concerns about the concentration of risk in domestic insurance and reinsurance markets. These concerns, along with concerns about pricing adequacy due to some insurers' practice of pricing below the pricing guidance, have led to a reduction in international reinsurance market appetite as insurers transfer most risk on a proportional basis. While the preferences have been largely removed, insurers have still faced challenges in accessing affordable reinsurance, including higher prices and higher retentions. In addition, the maximum retention requirement imposed by the insurance regulator, *Otoritas Jasa Keuangan* (OJK), means that the capacity of insurers to retain more risk is limited without raising further capital (and, as discussed below, OJK has increased the minimum capital requirements for all insurers which has also led to a need to raise capital).
- In Sri Lanka, challenges in accessing foreign currency during the economic crisis as well as some concerns about the quality of exposure data (i.e. data on insured structures) have had significant impacts on the appetite of reinsurers for assuming risk in Sri Lanka. In addition, premium prices have not increased much in recent years as insurers have focused instead on increased deductibles or coverage withdrawals, which has limited the attractiveness of assuming risk from Sri Lankan insurers (relative to other markets with higher pricing). The resulting reductions in reinsurance coverage have reportedly had an impact on insurer's willingness to provide coverage to households and businesses.

The contribution of national reinsurers to ensuring the availability of affordable reinsurance capacity has differed across countries. Malaysia Re usually assumes significantly more than the amount that insurers are required to cede and leads many of the reinsurance placements of Malaysian insurers. In the Philippines, Nat Re also assumes more than insurers are required to offer, particularly from smaller insurers, although capacity constraints limit its ability to accept more than 10% for larger placements. The national reinsurers in Indonesia are also significant sources of capacity and lead many placements by domestic insurers. This partly reflects efforts by OJK to enforce strict due diligence on foreign reinsurers, encourage diversification of reinsurance panels and prioritise placements with reinsurers that have strong credit ratios and a proven track record in paying valid claims to ceding insurers. The removal of preferences has led some foreign-owned insurance companies to cede risk to group reinsurance entities although many foreign reinsurers continue to transfer risk to the national reinsurers.

In Pakistan and Sri Lanka, the share of reinsurance placements that need to be offered to the national reinsurers are much higher and some insurers seem to be more reluctant to offer any more than what is required (although small insurers in Pakistan tend to cede more than is required to the national reinsurer). The national reinsurers in Pakistan and Sri Lanka tend to assume the share that insurers are required to offer. However, the National Insurance Trust Fund in Sri Lanka has faced some financial capacity constraints due to the impact of the foreign exchange crisis on its ability to access retrocession from international markets. The national reinsurer in Sri Lanka has also faced challenges due to the lack of an exemption from government procurement rules for placing retrocession, which has reduced retrocession market interest.

The national reinsurers in Indonesia, the Philippines and, in particular, Malaysia, have developed significant technical expertise and are increasingly competitive in the market. Malaysia Re, for example, is one of the largest reinsurers in Asia, is highly rated and assumes significant risk from insurers outside Malaysia. The national (and domestic) reinsurers in Indonesia and the national reinsurer in the Philippines are also increasingly competitive although their ability to compete for business internationally remains limited due to lower credit ratings and concerns about country concentration. The national reinsurers in Pakistan and Sri Lanka are perceived to be more akin to a government agency than an international or professional reinsurer. Some insurance companies in Pakistan and Sri Lanka raised concerns about counterparty risks due to their exposure to the national reinsurers. In Pakistan, some insurers indicated that their counterparty exposure to the (unrated) Pakistan Reinsurance Corporation had a negative impact on their own credit ratings. Neither the Pakistan Reinsurance Corporation nor the National Insurance Trust Fund in Sri Lanka are protected by an explicit government guarantee to assume any losses beyond the reinsurer's financial capacity.

Pricing by national reinsurers has tended to follow pricing trends in international markets. Therefore, none have been able to make any significant contribution to enhancing the affordability of reinsurance coverage. This results from the fact that most of the national reinsurers are partially listed (with profit-motivated shareholders), need to secure retrocession coverage (in some cases, significant)[21] and usually accept reinsurance placements together with other reinsurers.

In countries with significant takaful and other sharia-compliant insurance markets, limited availability of affordable retakaful (i.e. reinsurance based on sharia) could have an impact on the ability of takaful providers to provide financial protection to households and businesses. Retakaful capacity is much more limited than reinsurance capacity and a few stakeholders raised concerns about the limited availability of such capacity. In Malaysia, for example, there are only two domestic retakaful providers (including Malaysia Re) while concerns about the financial soundness of retakaful providers in some other countries limit the option for retakaful placements.

1.3. Policy, regulatory, supervisory and market approaches to addressing protection gaps in natural hazard insurance

1.3.1. Increasing demand for natural hazard insurance

Relatively more frequent experience with natural hazards across many countries in Asia has likely led to a higher level of risk perception than other parts of the world. However, in many countries in Asia, a higher level of risk perception has not translated into higher levels of insurance coverage for natural hazard losses. For example, in one survey of urban residents in Indonesia that had experienced climate-related extreme events, purchasing insurance was the least common among a set of preparedness actions (10.6% had acquired insurance and 6.8% were in the process of doing so – while 42.6% indicated that they were unlikely to purchase insurance in the future) (Adhi et al., 2019[16]). This divergence is likely driven, in part, by limited awareness of and trust in the value of insurance as a tool for providing financial protection.

Building insurance literacy

Improvements in insurance literacy can make an important contribution to addressing protection gaps in natural hazard insurance. A number of studies have found a positive correlation between the level of insurance literacy and the take-up of insurance. For example, one survey of Sri Lankan consumers found a positive correlation between insurance purchase and higher insurance literacy (along with higher levels of trust and perception of the benefits of insurance) (Weedige et al., 2019[65]). Similarly, a survey of consumers in India found that higher levels of insurance literacy increased the likelihood of acquiring micro-insurance (Uddin, 2017[66]).

Given the growing recognition of the importance of financial literacy, an increasing number of countries have established national financial literacy strategies, consistent with the OECD Recommendation on Financial Literacy (OECD, 2020[67]), or national financial inclusion strategies that include a component related to financial literacy. In some countries, the strategy has been established by a financial sector regulator, such as in Indonesia (OJK, 2021[25]) and Pakistan (State Bank of Pakistan, 2025[68])). The Central Bank of Sri Lanka has led the development of a National Financial Inclusion Strategy and a Financial Literacy Roadmap that includes the Insurance Regulatory Commission of Sri Lanka (and other government departments and agencies) as implementing agencies (Central Bank of Sri Lanka, 2021[69]; Central Bank of Sri Lanka, 2024[70]). In Malaysia and the Philippines, financial inclusion and/or financial literacy strategies have been developed by a committee or network of financial sector regulators and other government departments and agencies, including the agency responsible for insurance regulation (Financial Education Network, 2025[71]; Financial Inclusion Steering Committee, 2024[72]).

High levels of financial literacy do not always translate into higher levels of insurance literacy (Weedige et al., 2019[65]). Achieving insurance literacy requires an understanding of various elements essential to understanding the need for, role and scope of insurance coverage, including: (i) understanding exposure to risk; (ii) awareness of risk mitigation strategies; (iii) understanding of the concept of insurance, including the principles and benefits of insurance; (iv) understanding of the features of insurance products, and the rights and duties of the insured; and (v) awareness of how to find information on available insurance coverage and how to access it (based on (Weedige et al., 2019[65])). The OECD Recommendation on Financial Literacy also outlines some specific elements that need to be incorporated into financial literacy programmes in order to support insurance literacy, including a need to promote an understanding of risk, risk mitigation and the possible role of insurance as well as information and tools to support better use by individuals of insurance products (OECD, 2020[67]).

The national financial literacy and financial inclusion strategies in Indonesia, Malaysia, Pakistan, the Philippines and Sri Lanka place different levels of emphasis on insurance, relative to other financial services. In Malaysia and the Philippines, the strategies include objectives that are specifically targeted at "risk protection", including a focus on protection against natural hazard risks (Financial Education Network, 2025[71]; Financial Inclusion Steering Committee, 2024[72]). The objectives of the financial literacy strategy in Indonesia are not specific to a type of financial service although elements related to insurance and insurance literacy are integrated throughout the strategy. This includes specific questions on insurance product features, benefits, risks, costs, consumer rights and obligations and how to access insurance in order to measure insurance literacy through the periodic National Survey on Financial Literacy and Inclusion (SNLIK) (OJK, 2021[25]). OJK has also included a module on insurance within its Financial Education Learning Management System, a platform that provides a mechanism for independent learning and a repository for financial education materials (OJK, 2021[25]).

The national financial inclusion strategies in Pakistan and Sri Lanka, and the financial literacy roadmap in Sri Lanka, place more limited emphasis on insurance. In Pakistan, there is an objective to promote microinsurance and microtakaful in order to help create a conducive environment for the microfinance sector (State Bank of Pakistan, 2025[68]). In Sri Lanka, the national financial inclusion strategy appears to be mostly focused on credit access (Central Bank of Sri Lanka, 2021[69]), while insurance is seen as one of a number of the elements relevant to individuals' financial management in the financial literacy roadmap (Central Bank of Sri Lanka, 2024[70]).

The insurance regulators in Pakistan and Sri Lanka have developed online guides to support consumers' understanding of insurance. The Securities and Exchange Commission of Pakistan (SECP), through its investor education initiative, has published a basic guide to insurance that provides an overview of the principles of insurance and potential benefits, describes the different types of insurance and how to access coverage, and outlines the process for complaints, including the role of the SECP in the complaint process (Jama Punji, 2017[73]). The Insurance Regulatory Commission of Sri Lanka has published a booklet outlining the basic principles of insurance, describing the types of insurance and providing practical guidance on what to consider when acquiring insurance and avenues for resolving complaints (Insurance Board of Sri Lanka, 2019[74]). This is complemented by efforts to disseminate information about insurance and insurance concepts through social media channels as well as through print media, radio and television programmes and short messages sent to mobile phones.

Insurance associations and insurance companies also play a key role in supporting insurance literacy. The insurance associations in Indonesia (AAUI, 2018[75]), Malaysia (PIAM, 2025[76]), Pakistan (Insurance Association of Pakistan, n.d.[77]), the Philippines (PIRA, 2021[78]) and Sri Lanka (Ada derana Business, 2019[79]) have all identified increasing public awareness about insurance among their main objectives. The associations support awareness and educational campaigns, conferences and other types of events. In Indonesia, Pakistan and Sri Lanka, national insurance days have been established by – or with the support of – the insurance associations as a means of enhancing public awareness. Some associations have information for consumers on their websites, including information on insurance products and complaints and redress mechanisms. In the Philippines, the insurance association has developed "PIRA TV" which includes short videos in talk-show format on different types of insurance products, including fire insurance (PIRA, n.d.[80]). In Indonesia, financial service providers (including insurance companies) are required to conduct regular activities to improve financial literacy and inclusion and report on those activities to the regulator.

Building trust in insurance

A lack of trust in insurance as an effective form of financial protection is a potential driver of low insurance penetration in some countries and appears to be a challenge in Indonesia, Malaysia, Pakistan, the Philippines and Sri Lanka. Given the nature of insurance, as a promise of a future payment based on the occurrence of an uncertain event, trust that the provider of that promise will fulfil their contractual obligation is critical. Some studies have identified a direct relationship between levels of trust and the willingness to purchase intangible products such as insurance (Weedige et al., 2019[65]).

Trust in insurance may be impacted by low levels of financial literacy (Weedige et al., 2019[65]), a lack of experience with insurance, preconceived notions about being treated unfairly or about the financial capacity of insurance companies to meet their obligations, concerns about fraud or scams, or negative past experience with insurance (such as disputes or lengthy claims settlement processes (EIOPA, 2024[4])). For example, the OECD's 2024 Consumer Finance Risk Monitor found that issues related to claims handling and contractual clauses (including exclusions in coverage) were the most frequently identified drivers of complaints received by insurance firms, alternative dispute resolution mechanisms and supervisors in responding jurisdictions (OECD, 2024[81]).

Insurance regulators can make a number of contributions to building trust in insurance by responding to some of the drivers of mistrust. Many of these contributions relate to functions that are generally within the scope of insurance supervision, such as ensuring that the terms and conditions included in policy coverage are clear and easy to understand (including any coverage exclusions), premium pricing is not excessive, claims are settled quickly and that complaint and redress mechanisms are communicated to consumers and are effective in the resolution of disputes. A number of insurance supervisors also implement measures to ensure that consumers can find information on how to avoid potential fraud and scams, such as by publishing lists of licensed insurance companies and intermediaries and, in some cases, public notices about entities that are not authorised by the regulator. For example, the Insurance Regulatory Commission of Sri Lanka published a list of licensed insurance companies and intermediaries on its website and issues public notices to encourage the public to visit the website and learn about entities that are authorised by the Commission. Bank Negara Malaysia maintains a list of companies and websites that may be wrongly perceived as having been licensed or regulated by the regulator (Bank Negara Malaysia, 2025[82]).

Efforts to build public awareness of the role of the insurance regulator in monitoring the financial soundness of insurance companies could also support trust in the insurance sector. Policy makers have a role in supporting public awareness of the functions of insurance supervisors while also ensuring that insurance supervisors have sufficient powers and resources to undertake the functions that support trust in the insurance sector. Several countries have also established policyholder protection schemes which, as long as consumers are aware of – and understand the role of – such schemes, should also support consumer confidence that any valid claims will be paid (Box 1.3).

Box 1.3. Policyholder protection schemes

Policyholder protection schemes, which are sometimes referred to as insurance guarantee schemes, are arrangements to provide protection to policyholders in the event of a failure of an insurance company by either paying valid claims or providing funding for any shortfall in order to support the transfer of the failed insurer's business to another insurer (IAIS, 2023[83]). Policyholder protection schemes that provide protection for non-life insurance policyholders exist in a number of OECD countries (e.g. Australia, Canada, Denmark, France, Japan, Korea, Norway, the United Kingdom, the United States) (OECD, 2013[84]). A few schemes have also been established in non-OECD Asian countries, including in Malaysia (the Takaful and Insurance Benefits Protection System which provides 100% compensation up to MYR 500 000 for claims due to property insurance policyholders) (PIDM, 2025[85]), Singapore (which provides 100% compensation for claims due to property insurance policyholders up to SGD 300 000) (SDIC, 2018[86]; ASEAN Insurance Council, 2023[87]) and Thailand (which provides compensation for claims due to property insurance policyholders up to THB 1 million) (ASEAN Insurance Council, 2023[87]). In Indonesia, a Policy Guarantee Program is planned for implementation in 2028 although the scope of policies covered has not been announced (Asia Insurance Review, 2023[88]).

The existence of policyholder protection schemes, where disclosed to policyholders, can support confidence in the insurance sector (IAIS, 2023[83]; OECD, 2013[84]). A consultation paper by the European Insurance and Occupational Pensions Authority (EIOPA) on the harmonisation of insurance guarantee schemes suggested that the additional confidence in the insurance sector could lead to increased consumer demand for insurance products (EIOPA, 2019[89]). One rating agency has indicated that Indonesia's guarantee programme is likely to improve confidence in the insurance sector and support market growth (Pratiwi and Novaryani, 2022[90]).

Increasing take-up of property insurance penetration

Increasing the take-up of property insurance is essential for addressing protection gaps in natural hazard insurance. Coverage for natural hazard risks is usually attached to property insurance and households and businesses without property insurance will not be provided with an opportunity to acquire natural hazard insurance coverage. They would also have more limited access to any insurer efforts to raise awareness of the need for coverage against natural hazard risks. For example, in Sri Lanka, insurer awareness raising campaigns are sometimes limited to existing clients (i.e. households and businesses with an existing insurance coverage). There is a clear link between the level of property insurance penetration and the share of natural hazard losses that are insured. With only a few exceptions, a higher share of natural hazard losses is insured in countries with higher levels of property insurance penetration (Figure 1.16).

Figure 1.16. Property insurance penetration and insurance coverage for natural hazard losses

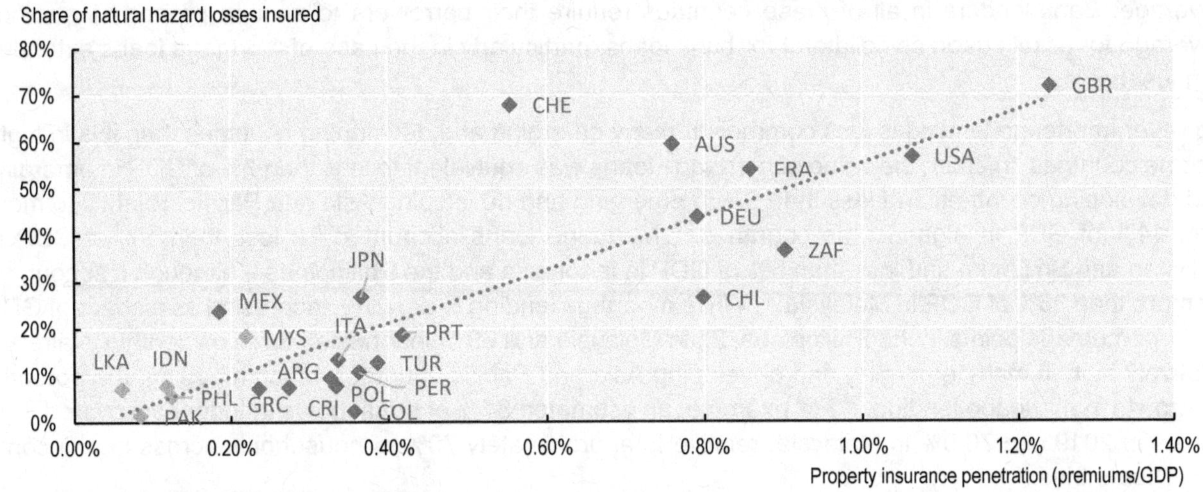

Source: OECD calculations based on data on insured and economic losses related to natural hazards provided by Swiss Re (Swiss Re, sigma database. All rights reserved.), data on property insurance premiums reported in OECD (2025[48]), SECP (2024[55]), Insurance Commission (2023[53]), IRCSL (2024[59]) and GDP data from IMF (2024[91]).

In addition to insurance literacy and trust, there are a number of other factors that can influence the level of property insurance penetration. For example, one study examined the correlation between insurance density (premiums per capita) in approximately 40 developed and emerging markets and a range of factors related to income, probability of loss, risk awareness, cost of insurance and legal protections for property rights - and found positive links between insurance density, income, probability of loss and property rights protection (Esho et al., 2004[92]). Figure 1.17 illustrates the positive correlation between property insurance penetration and per capita income levels and property rights protection.

Figure 1.17. Property rights, income and property insurance penetration

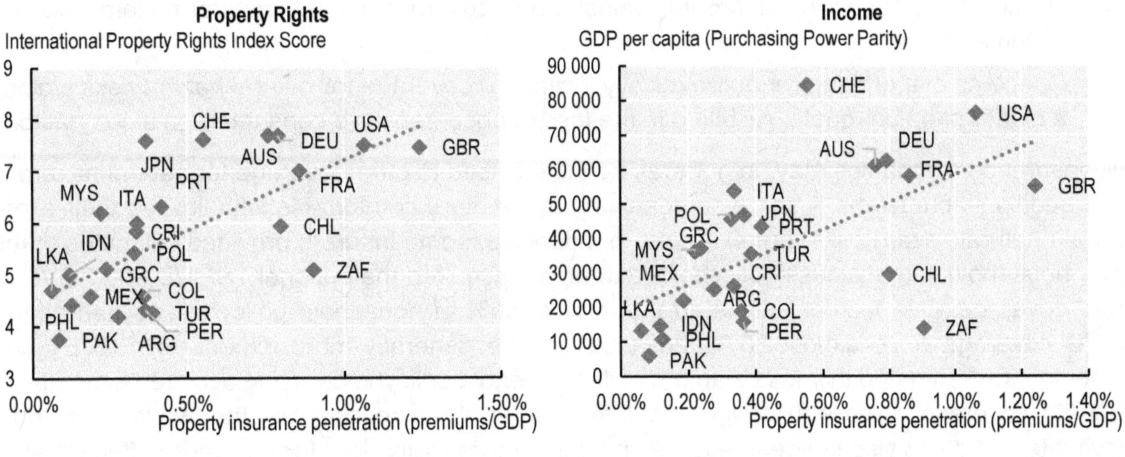

Source: OECD calculations based on Property Rights Index Scores provided by Property Rights Alliance (2024[93]), data on property insurance premiums reported in OECD (2025[48]), SECP (2024[55]), Insurance Commission (2023[53]), IRCSL (2024[59]) and GDP and GDP per capita data from IMF (2024[91]).

In many countries bank lenders play an important role in distributing and often effectively mandating the purchase of property insurance among their borrowers. This is the case in Indonesia, Malaysia, Pakistan, the Philippines and Sri Lanka. The insurance supervisors, insurance companies and intermediaries in these five countries all indicated that bank lenders are a major driver of the take-up of property insurance coverage. Bank lenders in all of these countries require their borrowers to acquire property insurance coverage for assets used as collateral for bank loans, particularly in the case of mortgage loans extended to households.

However, mortgage lending is less common in many emerging and developing countries than it is in high-income countries. In 2021, the value of mortgage loans was equivalent to less than 7% of GDP in emerging and developing countries and less than 9% in emerging and developing Asia and Pacific, relative to more than 44% of GDP in high-income countries.[22] Mortgage loans accounted for less than 1% of GDP in Pakistan and Sri Lanka and less than 5% of GDP in Indonesia and the Philippines – although it accounted for more than 35% of GDP in Malaysia.[23] While mortgage lending is growing, increasing as a share of GDP by 11 percentage points in the Philippines, 23 in Malaysia and 69 in Indonesia, home ownership is already relatively high in many emerging and developing Asia and Pacific countries which may limit the potential for growth in mortgage lending.[24] For example, an estimated 84% of households in Indonesia owned their homes in 2019 and 76.9% in Malaysia, relative to approximately 70% of households across high-income OECD countries.[25]

Encouraging take-up of coverage for natural hazard risks

Insurers take different approaches to offering coverage for natural hazard risks in different countries, ranging from an automatic inclusion of coverage for these risks in property insurance to an optional add-on of coverage for natural hazard risks. The approach taken to offering coverage can have important implications on the magnitude of protection gaps. Where it is optional for insurers to offer coverage for natural hazard risks, some insurers may choose not to offer coverage for these risks, or for specific types of natural hazards, to households and businesses, whether due to:

- Uncertainty related to the exposure that they would be assuming by offering coverage, possibly due to gaps in the availability of quality data on hazards or exposure, or the potential for climate change to lead to increased losses.
- The potential magnitude of natural hazard risk in particular high-risk locations or communities.
- Difficulties in accessing affordable reinsurance coverage for the natural hazard risks that they assume.
- Concerns that offering (or automatically including) coverage for natural hazard risks would lead to a higher premium quote, resulting in the loss of price-sensitive consumers to a competitor.

While insurance companies may, in general, be incentivised to offer coverage for natural hazard risk and collect additional premiums,[26] some companies may be more comfortable with limiting their exposure to uncertain natural hazard risks. For example, in Indonesia, some insurers provided estimates of the share of their household and business policyholders that had acquired the optional TSFWD and EQVET natural hazard coverage. One insurer estimated that almost 80% of household policyholders had acquired the TSFWD coverage while almost 30% had acquired (the generally more expensive) EQVET coverage. Another insurer estimated that less than 5% of its household policyholders had acquired either the TSFWD or EQVET coverage.[27] While this might result from other differences among the two insurers' portfolio of policyholders, it could also suggest that one insurer is more willing to offer – or more effective at selling – the optional natural hazard coverage than the other.

In some cases, practices vary across different insurance companies within the same country. For example, in Pakistan, some insurers reportedly include coverage for natural hazards automatically with household property insurance coverage while others only offer it as an optional additional coverage. In Sri Lanka, insurance companies can choose to exclude coverage for specific types of natural hazard risks. Where insurers take different approaches to the inclusion of this coverage, households and businesses may be confused by what is covered in the policies offered by different insurers, although clear policy documents may help to avoid potential confusion if there is an adequate level of insurance literacy. Differences in, and potential complexity of, products can make it more difficult for consumers to compare between the offerings of different insurance companies. It could also exacerbate efforts to improve trust in insurance as an effective form of financial protection should policyholders learn that a loss is unexpectedly not covered.

Offering coverage for natural hazard risks as a standard or automatic inclusion in household and business property insurance, even with an option to opt-out, can ensure that insurance companies are offering coverage and that households and businesses are given an option to acquire that coverage. A mandatory offer of insurance coverage for natural hazard risks could also respond to some of the challenges to enhancing take-up identified above, by:

- Ensuring that consumers are aware of the availability of coverage for natural hazard risks.
- Reducing the possibility that consumers will mistakenly assume that coverage for natural hazard risks is included in basic (property) fire insurance.
- Providing insurers (or intermediaries) with a (mandated) opportunity to build awareness of natural hazard risks and the benefits of - and need for – specific insurance coverage, given that insurers would be required to explain the coverage and its benefits and limits to policyholders.

The automatic inclusion or mandatory offer, with an opt-out option for consumers, will not fully address protection gaps if consumers choose not to take-up coverage for natural hazard risks or acquire any property insurance at all. Some insurance supervisors, intermediaries and/or insurance companies in Indonesia, Malaysia, Pakistan, the Philippines and Sri Lanka (and elsewhere) have suggested going further and requiring households and/or businesses to acquire property insurance that covers natural hazard risks (i.e. mandatory purchase). In Indonesia, for example, recent legislation on the Development and Strengthening of the Financial Sector authorises the government to establish mandatory insurance programmes for specific segments of the population and lines of business, including household insurance against disaster risks (Government of Indonesia, 2023[94]).

While mandatory purchase, automatic inclusion and mandatory offer of natural hazard coverage have tended to reduce protection gaps (Figure 1.18), these approaches can also create challenges for insurers and policyholders. For insurers, all three approaches create an obligation to offer coverage for risks that they might not have the capacity or appetite to assume and could lead them to not offer any property insurance coverage to households, businesses or entire communities that have high-levels of exposure to one or more natural hazards.[28] For policyholders, mandatory purchase could be perceived as a tax and could force them to purchase coverage that they cannot afford.[29] Similarly, automatic inclusion of coverage for natural hazard risks could lead to premiums that are unaffordable for some households and businesses and lead them to choose to not acquire any property insurance at all. As discussed below, in countries where coverage is mandatory, natural hazard coverage is automatically included, or where insurers are required to offer coverage, some form of public-private insurance programme is often in place to support insurance availability and affordability.

Figure 1.18. The impact of automatically including flood insurance coverage on protection gaps

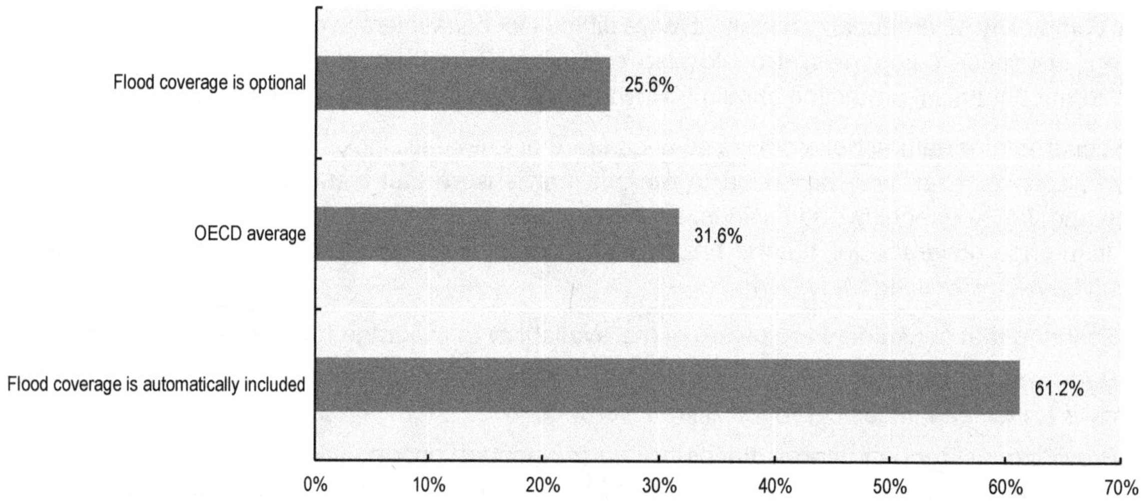

Source: OECD calculations based on data provided by Swiss Re (Swiss Re, sigma database. All rights reserved.).

Banks in many countries require borrowers to acquire insurance coverage. The insurance requirements are usually imposed voluntarily by banks as a means to reduce the risk that the value of their collateral will decline as a result of property damage. As a result, there may be inconsistencies in approach as banks may or may not require coverage for natural hazard risks - and may invest more or less effort into ensuring that borrowers maintain their coverage over the life of the loan. Banks in Malaysia, the Philippines and Sri Lanka (for some hazards) tend to require their borrowers to acquire coverage for natural hazard risks, although some insurers in Malaysia indicated that this requirement is not imposed universally by banks. In Sri Lanka, one insurance sector stakeholder noted that banks usually do not monitor whether a borrower renews their coverage in subsequent years. In Indonesia, most banks do not require coverage for natural hazard risks although some banks have recently started to impose this requirement. In Pakistan, banks are required by legislation to ensure that borrowers have property insurance although this requirement does not extend to coverage for natural hazard risks.

While bank-imposed requirements for natural hazard insurance coverage can lead to many of the same challenges for insurers and policyholders as other requirements on insurance purchase or offer, there are likely other benefits in reducing banking sector exposure to natural hazard risks that should be taken into account. Significant protection gaps could create risks to the broader financial system if a major event leads to substantial defaults among uninsured households and businesses. Ensuring that banks require their borrowers to have coverage against natural hazard risks for the properties used as collateral could limit this risk. Reducing the risk that natural hazards lead to broader financial system stress has become an increasing focus for many financial sector policy makers and regulators around the world (Poeschl, 2022[95]; Kauko et al., 2021[96]; Newman, Adams-Kane and Nicholls, 2023[97]; European Central Bank and European Systemic Risk Board, 2023[98]; Allen et al., 2023[99]; Bank of England, 2019[100]; Kahn, Panjwani and Santos, 2024[101]).

In most countries, including in Indonesia, Malaysia, Pakistan, the Philippines and Sri Lanka, the approach to providing natural hazard insurance coverage is determined by insurance market practice (i.e. insurers decide whether coverage for specific natural hazards is included with – or must be added to – property insurance coverage offered to households and businesses).[30] However, insurance supervisors generally have a role in establishing rules or principles to be applied by insurers in their conduct of business, which includes ensuring proper disclosures and documentation on coverage and exclusions. In the context of increasing climate-related risks, the International Association of Insurance Supervisors has proposed that supervisors' Conduct of Business requirements (Insurance Core Principle 19) should: (i) ensure that information on natural hazard coverage and exclusions is clearly stated in "disclosures, advertising materials, pre-contractual and contractual documentation"; (ii) encourage insurers to develop a common approach to presenting insurance options and different types of coverage to consumers; and (iii) undertake testing to confirm consumer understanding of coverage exclusions (IAIS, 2025[102]). Some insurance supervisors plan to take steps on these issues. For example, the Securities and Exchange Commission of Pakistan plans to introduce standardised retail policy documents (SECP, 2024[103]). Some insurance companies (e.g. Sri Lanka) suggested a need for the insurance regulator to encourage further standardisation of coverage and improved disclosure of exclusions.

Ultimately, the decision on whether to intervene requires an assessment of the potential risks of mandating an approach to offering coverage for insurers and consumers relative to the potential benefits in reducing protection gaps. Some insurers, particularly in Malaysia and the Philippines, indicated some progress in enhancing the take-up of insurance coverage for natural hazard risks as a result of increasing risk awareness and (unfortunately) more frequent experience of the impact of natural hazards.

Expanding reach and offering suitable and affordable coverage

Progress in addressing protection gaps in natural hazard insurance will also require efforts to expand the reach of available and affordable insurance coverage, including by: (i) leveraging available distribution channels; and (ii) developing coverage options that are suitable for – and attractive to – segments of the population that have traditionally been uninsured or financially excluded.

Leveraging distribution channels

Insurance coverage for property and natural hazards may be sold through a variety of distribution channels, including through direct sales by insurance companies or through intermediaries such as agents, brokers and banks (bancassurance). Brokers and agents, including agents representing multiple insurers and those representing a single insurer, account for the largest share of non-life insurance sales in most countries (Figure 1.19). In general, households and smaller businesses tend to access coverage through direct sales, agents and banks, while larger businesses tend to access insurance markets through brokers.

While accounting for a small share of non-life insurance distribution in most countries, sales through banking and digital channels have increased and are expected to account for an increasing share of non-life insurance distribution in the future.

Non-life insurance distribution through banks accounts for a relatively minor share of non-life insurance distribution in the Philippines and Sri Lanka, and particularly in Pakistan, despite the significance of bancassurance in driving take-up among households (given the link to mortgage lending). In other parts of the world, bancassurance has reportedly been one of the fastest-growing distribution channels and now accounts for almost 10% of non-life insurance distribution in Europe and 25% in some Latin American markets (McKinsey & Company (Insurance Practice), 2024[104]).

Figure 1.19. Non-life insurance distribution channels

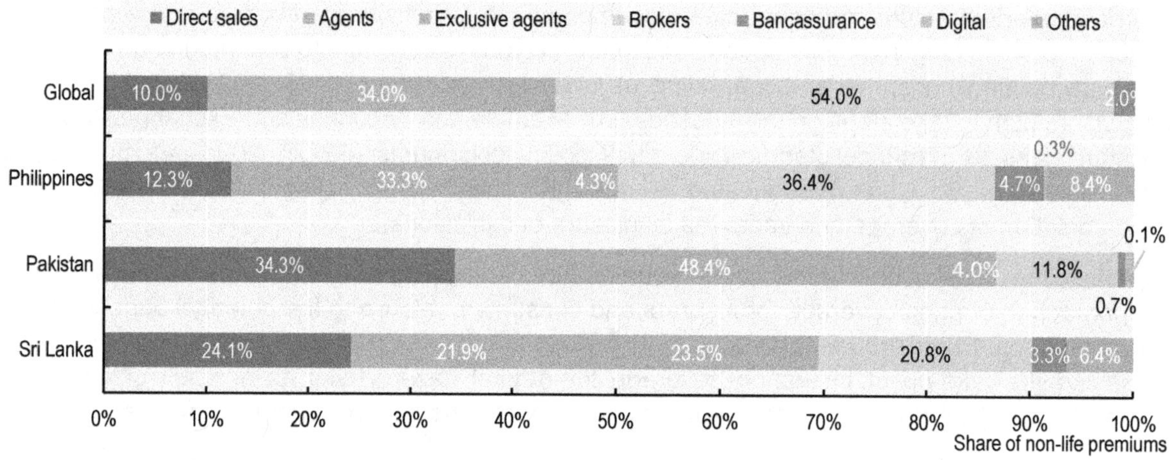

Note: Exclusive agents are classified as "general agents" in the Philippines and as "corporate agents" in Pakistan. The "digital" category includes "e-commerce, online and digital sales" in the Philippines and telcos, websites and web aggregators in Pakistan (this category was not available in Sri Lanka). For the global data, "Direct sales" includes other channels (other than agents, brokers and bancassurance) while "Agents" includes only tied agents and branches. Global data is for 2018. Data for Malaysia and Indonesia was not available.
Source: OECD based on data on distribution channels from IRCSL (2022[58]), Insurance Commission (2023[53]), SECP (2024[55]), McKinsey & Company (Insurance Practice) (2021[105]).

It is likely that opportunities exist to increase the contribution of bancassurance to distributing property and natural hazard insurance coverage in Indonesia, Malaysia, Pakistan, the Philippines, Sri Lanka and other emerging and developing Asia and Pacific countries. Access to and use of banking services is increasing across Asia, with approximately 50% of individuals in Indonesia and the Philippines reporting having an account (either their own or shared) with a bank or other financial institution in 2021, and close to 90% in Malaysia and Sri Lanka (although only 16% reported having an account in Pakistan) (World Bank, 2023[106]). In addition, increasingly local access to a financial institution means that only about 25% of individuals in Indonesia, Pakistan and the Philippines – and less than 2% of individuals in Malaysia and Sri Lanka – indicated that distance to access a bank or financial institution is a reason for not having an account (World Bank, 2023[106]) (Figure 1.20). Distribution of coverage through banks might also reduce some of the challenges related to mistrust in insurance. For example, in Indonesia, one survey found that over 80% of respondents have confidence in banks, relative to approximately 10% that have confidence in the insurance sector (OJK, 2021[25]). Bancassurance could also provide a means to enhance coverage among SMEs given that many will have an existing relationship with a bank (Ingram, 2025[107]).

Figure 1.20. Access to banking services

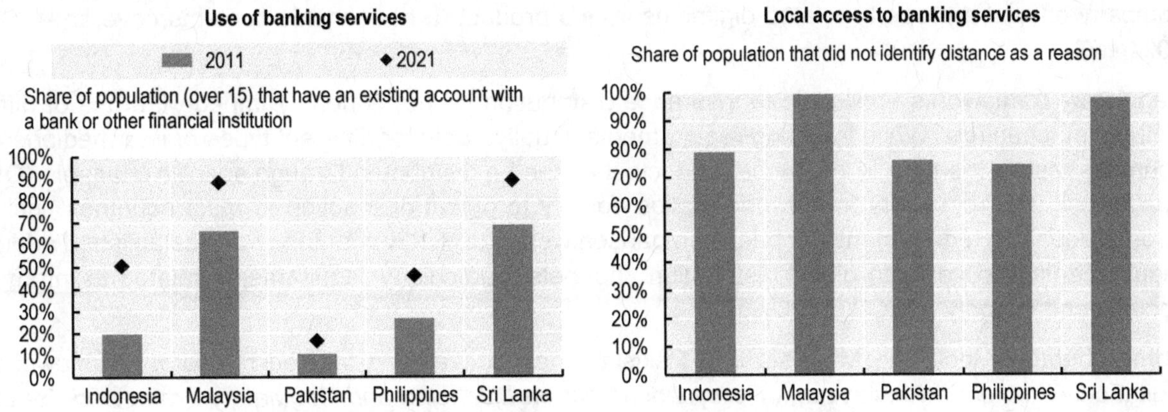

Source: World Bank (2023[106]), The Global Findex Database 2021: Financial Inclusion, Digital Payments, and Resilience in the Age of COVID-19, https://www.worldbank.org/en/publication/globalfindex.

Growing access to and use of technology provides new opportunities for digital distribution of insurance coverage. The (vast) majority of the population in emerging and developing Asia and Pacific countries have access to the internet and own mobile phones (Figure 1.21), providing an opportunity to greatly expand the distribution of insurance coverage through digital sales channels. In Europe and Australia, for example, digital sales (including digital bancassurance) account for approximately 30% of non-life premiums (McKinsey & Company (Insurance Practice), 2024[104]).

Figure 1.21. Access to the internet and mobile phones

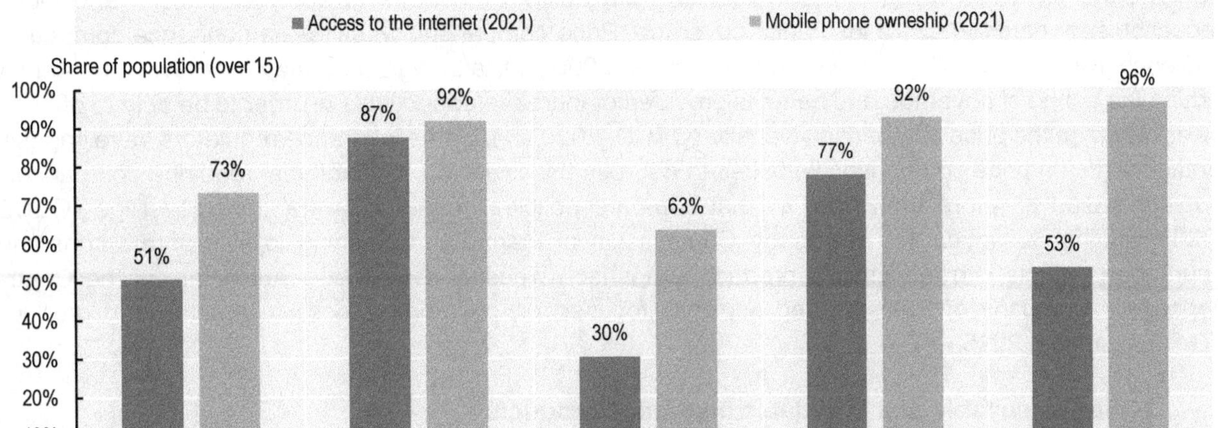

Source: World Bank (2023[106]), The Global Findex Database 2021: Financial Inclusion, Digital Payments, and Resilience in the Age of COVID-19, https://www.worldbank.org/en/publication/globalfindex.

The distribution of non-life insurance coverage through digital channels, such as via direct internet-based sales or through price comparison websites, remains limited - accounting for less than 1% of all non-life premiums collected in both Pakistan and the Philippines (data for this distribution channel was not available for the other countries). In Pakistan, for example, a recent survey undertaken by the Securities and Exchange Commission of Pakistan found that less than half of insurance companies offered products through digital channels and that the impact of third-party digital platforms (such as price comparison websites) was minimal. Digital products were available for only a few lines of business and only one company offered a property-related digital insurance product (a households contents coverage) (SECP, 2024[108]).

Regulatory frameworks applicable to insurance distribution do not generally impede the use of different distribution channels. While licensing requirements usually apply for different types of intermediaries, few countries restrict the type of insurance products that can be distributed through specific channels (OECD, 2020[109]).[31] The regulatory framework applies equally to digital distribution in most countries, including through licensing requirements for price comparison websites. A few countries have established additional requirements applicable to digital distribution channels, particularly requirements related to information security and integrity (OECD, 2020[109]).

Some countries, including Malaysia and Pakistan, have developed tailored regulatory frameworks for digital-only insurers. In Malaysia, a *Policy Document on Licensing and Regulatory Framework for Digital Insurers and Takaful Operators (DITOs)* was issued in July 2024. The framework provides a tailored licensing and regulatory framework, including a lower minimum capital requirement during a limited foundational phase, to facilitate the entry of insurers and takaful providers that deliver their products digitally and aim to deliver strong and meaningful value propositions related to inclusion, competition and efficiency (Bank Negara Malaysia, 2024[110]). The Securities and Exchange Commission of Pakistan introduced a registration framework for digital-only insurers in August 2022, along with a framework for dedicated microinsurers (see below), with the aim of encouraging innovation, expanding the range of available products and supporting financial inclusion. Similar to the framework in Malaysia, digital-only insurers can benefit from lower minimum capital requirements (SECP, 2024[108]). While these frameworks aim to encourage the establishment of digital insurers rather than promote digital distribution, digital insurers would normally distribute their products through digital channels.

Regulators should monitor the use and impact of price comparison websites given the highly competitive markets, the price-sensitivity of consumers and the ability of insurers to apply exclusions and higher deductibles for natural hazard insurance coverage. Price comparison websites can enhance competition and encourage affordability (Brown and Goolsbee, 2000[111]), although they may incentivise insurers to reduce the scope of coverage and benefits provided or increase deductibles in order to be able to offer the lowest price on the price comparison website (OECD, 2020[109]). Some insurance regulators have imposed requirements on price comparison websites to address this issue by, for example, requiring comparisons that are based on more than price or that compare policies based on a standard coverage (OECD, 2020[109]). The Securities and Exchange Commission of Pakistan is planning to incorporate consumer insurance products into the Emlaak product comparison website, owned by a subsidiary of the Central Depository Company of Pakistan and currently focused on providing access to mutual fund products (ITMinds Limited, 2025[112]).

Offering suitable and affordable insurance products

Offering suitable and affordable natural hazard insurance coverage options that are attractive to the households and small businesses that are excluded from the existing insurance market[32] will also be critical in reducing protection gaps for natural hazard risks. This could include products that offer more basic levels of coverage, including microinsurance or a basic natural hazard insurance coverage, innovative products that provide coverage based on parametric triggers as well as products that respond to religious and cultural beliefs and customs, such as takaful and other sharia-compliant financial protection products.

Microinsurance

Microinsurance generally refers to insurance coverage that is offered to low-income households or micro and small enterprises and that provides a small amount of coverage for a low premium cost.

Microinsurance products have been developed to protect against a broad range of risks, including for agricultural risks, health, accident, life, credit as well as to protect property.

Insurance companies offer a variety of microinsurance products targeted to low-income households and small businesses, including products that provide coverage for natural hazard risks. In Pakistan and Sri Lanka, some insurers have introduced microinsurance schemes that provide a basic level of coverage against natural hazards to low-income households and small businesses – sometimes in partnership with other organisations such as microfinance providers or rural support programmes. In Indonesia, the insurance associations and some individual insurers have developed microinsurance products for natural hazards (and specific products for volcano and earthquake) as well as for property-related risks more generally (Biese et al., 2023[113]). One reinsurer in Indonesia has also been developing a proposal for a microinsurance coverage for natural hazard risks to be distributed more broadly. In Malaysia, some insurers have introduced microinsurance coverage against natural hazard risks for low-income households, although take-up has been limited.

However, the availability and take-up of microinsurance coverage for property and natural hazard risks is much more limited than for other types of coverage, such as life, credit and health. For example, one global examination of available microinsurance products found that less than 2% of the microinsurance premiums written in 2023 were for non-agriculture property products (Merry and Rozo Calderon, 2025[114]). Microinsurance coverage for property and natural hazard risks is also limited in emerging and developing Asia and Pacific countries. Property-related products reportedly account for only a small share of the microinsurance market in Indonesia (approximately 5%) (Ismail, Sivarajah and Chow, 2020[115]). In Pakistan, microinsurance for property risks accounted for less than 0.1% of the 12.5 million microinsurance policies in force in 2022 (SECP, 2024[116]). In the Philippines, which is among the largest microinsurance markets in the world, the vast majority of coverage (95%) is for life (including credit) and health risks (Insurance Asia, 2025[117]; Ismail, Sivarajah and Chow, 2020[115]).

While the number of individuals covered by microinsurance and the amount of premiums collected have increased[33] and are expected to continue to increase,[34] the broadening of microinsurance, for property as well as other risks, has faced several challenges. These include challenges in identifying cost-effective distribution channels, a lack of demand and difficulties in achieving financial sustainability, particularly where initial subsidies are withdrawn. Some insurers in Malaysia indicated that microinsurance products have faced high loss ratios, although the average claims ratio for property-related microinsurance is reportedly low on a global basis (generally below 25% in recent years (Merry and Rozo Calderon, 2025[114]; Merry and Rozo Calderon, 2023[118])). In some countries, premium taxes or value-added taxes are applied on an equivalent basis to microinsurance products which could limit the financial viability of these products. For example, in the Philippines, taxes applicable to non-life insurance products can account for more than 20% of the premium charged for microinsurance coverage (Asian Development Bank, 2024[119]). The Securities and Exchange Commission of Pakistan has also raised concerns about the impact of taxes on the affordability of microinsurance products (SECP, 2024[116]).

A greater diversification of distribution channels and broader use of digital distribution channels could help improve the financial viability of microinsurance for property risks. The vast majority (90%) of property-related microinsurance products in Asia-Pacific are distributed through agents and brokers and microfinance institutions (Merry and Rozo Calderon, 2025[114]). Digital distribution accounts for about 8% of microinsurance premiums (for all types of coverage) in Indonesia and only 3% in the Philippines (Ismail, Sivarajah and Chow, 2020[115]). There might also be opportunities to improve distribution and increase take-up by bundling property and natural hazard risk protection with other forms of coverage, particularly with life, credit and/or health coverage, given the more significant microinsurance penetration for these types of products. For example, in Samoa, an innovative coverage has been developed to provide a bundled protection against a number of natural hazard risks (cyclones, earthquakes, excess rainfall and drought) with a parametric trigger and additional benefits paid out on an indemnity basis for funeral, personal accident, hospital stays, house fire and term life (Chanel and Singh, 2025[120]).

Adaptations to the regulatory framework for microinsurance providers, or a specific regulatory framework for microinsurance, can help overcome some of the challenges related to the financial viability of microinsurance products. Tailored regulatory frameworks have been developed in Indonesia, Malaysia, Pakistan and the Philippines (and a framework is under development in Sri Lanka) (Merry and Rozo Calderon, 2023[118]):

- In Indonesia, regulations issued in 2015 and 2017 provide a definition of microinsurance and provide requirements aimed at ensuring that microinsurance products are simple, affordable and provide quick payment for valid claims (Biese et al., 2023[113]).
- In Pakistan, specific rules on the licensing of microinsurance providers and the launch of microinsurance products were implemented by the Securities and Exchange Commission of Pakistan in 2014 (SECP, 2024[116]). A recent report on the microinsurance landscape identified a number of remaining impediments to the growth of microinsurance and proposals for further regulatory adaptations, including the removal of unnecessary product approvals, an easing of agent qualification and a review of rules pertaining to bank distribution (SECP, 2024[116]). The Securities and Exchange Commission of Pakistan also provided a temporary reduction in capital requirements for microinsurance providers (along with digital-only insurers, as noted above) (SECP, 2024[116]).
- In the Philippines, a first circular defining microinsurance and the basic provisions of microinsurance products was issued in 2006 and was enhanced and amended by a set of regulations for the provision of microinsurance products that was issued in 2010. Further guidance on issues such as alternative dispute resolution mechanisms for microinsurance, distribution channels and performance standards has also been developed. In 2013, a legislative amendment to the Insurance Code was made to recognise microinsurance as a product that meets the risk protection needs of poorer segments of society and to establish maximum premiums and sums insured applicable to microinsurance (Insurance Commission, n.d.[121]). In January 2025, the Insurance Commission released a set of guidelines on inclusive microinsurance products aimed at further strengthening the effectiveness of microinsurance in meeting the protection needs of the poor (Insurance Commission, 2025[122]).
- In Malaysia, the *Perlindungan Tenang* initiative, initiated in 2021, has been established to enhance the availability of microinsurance and microtakaful products to meet the needs of unserved and underserved segments of the population (Bank Negara Malaysia, 2021[123]). It provides a set of requirements that insurance and takaful products must meet to qualify under the initiative, focused on affordability, accessibility, protection value, understandability and ease of use. It also offered some flexibilities in terms of product combinations (e.g. insurance coverage combined with financing) (Bank Negara Malaysia, 2021[123]). Government-provided vouchers that substantially reduced the cost of *Perlindungan Tenang* products were initially offered to support take-up and were reportedly successful in improving awareness of the value of insurance and takaful products among vulnerable segments of the population.

Basic natural hazard coverage

Coverage for natural hazard risks can account for a substantial portion of the premium for property insurance coverage, particularly in higher-risk areas. To support affordability, insurers could potentially offer a more basic or limited coverage for natural hazard risks as part of property insurance coverage (i.e. where the sum insured in the case of a natural hazard loss is lower than the sum insured for other types of covered risks, such as fire). In Malaysia, to address low take-up of (relatively costly) coverage for flood risks, insurers have proposed the automatic inclusion of a basic (limited) first-loss coverage for flood risk in all property insurance policies. A basic coverage for flood risk could be provided at a lower premium cost and could therefore encourage more households and businesses to acquire coverage for flood risk. Under the proposal, policyholders would be able to acquire full coverage for flood risk for an additional premium and also to opt-out of the basic coverage.

Automatically providing a basic or limited coverage at a more affordable cost could be effective in encouraging greater take-up of coverage for natural hazard risks among lower-income (or price-sensitive) households and businesses and could help insurers establish a broader and more diversified pool of natural hazard risks. However, there is also a risk that it could create confusion among policyholders about their coverage for these risks, particularly if insurers take different approaches when offering basic and comprehensive coverage. As in the case of varying deductibles for natural hazard risks, a basic coverage could also have negative implications for consumer trust if many policyholders face losses above the level of the basic coverage provided.

Parametric insurance

Parametric insurance is a type of coverage that is triggered by the occurrence of an event that meets or exceeds a pre-defined threshold, such as water level, wind speed, precipitation amount or earthquake magnitude – and makes payments of a fixed amount, regardless of the magnitude of losses incurred by the policyholder. Offering insurance coverage based on a parametric trigger can potentially support affordability by reducing underwriting and loss adjustment costs. It can also potentially offer faster post-event claims payouts, which can support quicker recovery and reduce the overall impact of natural hazard events. Microinsurance products often incorporate a parametric trigger (particularly for agricultural risks) although parametric triggers can also be applied as a complement (and possibly an alternative) to traditional indemnity-based property insurance coverage.

The offering of insurance coverage based on parametric triggers is limited in most countries although some studies project significant opportunities for growth.[35] Coverage for natural hazard risks (including property and agriculture risks) reportedly accounts for a significant share (70%) of the parametric insurance market (Global Market Insights, 2025[124]). The increasing availability of new data sources, such as earth observation imagery, data from connected devices, as well as enhanced capacities to analyse these new sources of data and automate underwriting, pricing and claims decisions could support the expansion of parametric insurance options (OECD, 2023[125]).

Some insurance companies in Indonesia have developed parametric insurance coverage for earthquake risk as well as products for weather-related risks targeted at agricultural producers. In Pakistan, some parametric products have been launched on a pilot basis to cover agricultural risks. In the Philippines, some insurers are exploring parametric products for natural hazard risks although no products have been broadly introduced to the market. Insurance companies in Sri Lanka noted a limited availability of parametric insurance coverage.

In some countries, insurance legislation or regulation can impede the ability of insurance companies to offer coverage based on parametric triggers. For example, there may be a legislative or regulatory definition of insurance that is tied to the indemnification of specific losses that could place parametric insurance outside the scope of what is considered insurance (Garcia Ocampo and Lopez Moreira, 2024[126]). Legislation and regulation have not impeded the offering of parametric insurance in Indonesia, Malaysia, Pakistan, the Philippines or Sri Lanka.

In a few jurisdictions, specific legal or regulatory frameworks have been developed to support the offering of parametric insurance, including in Argentina, Colombia, Puerto Rico, Uganda and Uruguay (Garcia Ocampo and Lopez Moreira, 2024[126]). In Chile, a legislative amendment in a 2023 FinTech law allowed for the offering of parametric insurance and mandated the development of regulations to establish conditions for offering parametric insurance and identify the types of risks that can be covered by parametric insurance (Comisión para el Mercado Financiero, 2024[127]). In the US state of New York, the state insurance law was amended in 2024 to allow for the offering of parametric insurance to protect against the occurrence of weather-related events and to include requirements for mandatory disclosures when distributing parametric insurance policies (Lema, 2025[128]).

Takaful and other sharia-compliant forms of financial protection

Takaful is a form of insurance based on sharia that operates as a pool funded by the contributions of participants which is used to make payouts to those impacted by a loss. The takaful provider receives a pre-agreed fee to cover the costs of operating the pool although any surplus belongs to the participants in the pool, not the takaful provider. In countries with significant Muslim populations, supporting the availability of takaful and other sharia-compliant financial protection products could potentially support higher take-up given the higher levels of trust in takaful products, relative to insurance (as highlighted above).

Takaful and other sharia-compliant forms of financial protection against property and natural hazard risks are broadly available in Indonesia, Malaysia and Pakistan and increasingly available in the Philippines. In 2023, takaful and sharia-compliant products accounted for 4% of the overall non-life market in Indonesia (OJK, 2024[129]), 11% in Pakistan (SECP, 2024[55]) and just over 20% in Malaysia (Bank Negara Malaysia, 2024[130]; Bank Negara Malaysia, 2024[131]). Specific frameworks have been developed in Indonesia, Malaysia, Pakistan and the Philippines. In Malaysia, for example, there is a specific legislative framework (*Islamic Financial Services Act*) outlining the requirements for providers of takaful coverage (as well as other Islamic financial services) which is supplemented by a *Takaful Operational Framework* guideline established by Bank Negara Malaysia in 2019 (Bank Negara Malaysia, 2019[132]). In the Philippines, a regulatory framework was recently issued to provide guidance to insurers wishing to establish a Takaful window (Insurance Commission, 2024[133]). A lack of takaful was identified as a barrier to take-up among some segments of the population in Sri Lanka.

Some insurance and other regulators have implemented measures to support the growth of takaful and sharia-compliant insurance. In Indonesia, sharia insurers have lower minimum capital requirements than conventional insurers (Norton Rose Fulbright, 2024[134]). In Pakistan, the banking sector is required to become fully sharia-compliant by 2028, which is expected to lead to an increase in the take-up of takaful, particularly when distributed by the banking sector. However, as noted above, limited global retakaful capacity could create challenges to the expansion of takaful coverage for natural hazard risks. Bank Negara Malaysia has committed to working with the reinsurance and retakaful industry to build the necessary capacity to meet the risk transfer needs of the domestic insurance and takaful sectors (Bank Negara Malaysia, 2022[135]). The Securities and Exchange Commission of Pakistan is considering the potential role of a pooling arrangement in enhancing retakaful capacity (SECP, 2024[136]).

1.3.2. Enhancing insurance sector appetite and capacity for natural hazard risks

Improving data quality and the availability of risk assessment tools

Quality data on hazards, exposure (i.e. buildings) and vulnerability (i.e. structural resilience), as well as the capacity to analyse that data through risk assessment tools such as catastrophe models, is critical for underwriting and pricing insurance coverage for natural hazard risks. The quality of data and models impacts the willingness of insurers to underwrite coverage, their ability to charge premiums based on risk and their access to affordable reinsurance coverage, particularly proportional reinsurance.

Governments play a key role in providing risk data and assessment tools, such as hazard and risk maps for different natural hazards, data on past flood inundation levels as well as information on existing protective infrastructure such as flood barriers. Some governments have invested significantly in developing quality data and risk assessment tools and make this information broadly available for use by insurance companies and the broader public. For example, in the Philippines, the government has launched a multi-agency initiative to provide a centralised source of information on natural hazard risks, delivered through the *Hazard Hunter Philippines* software application. The application allows insurers (and the public) to generate hazard assessment reports for specific geographical locations and insurance companies have been encouraged by the Insurance Commission to use this tool in assessing natural hazard risks and underwriting coverage (Insurance Commission, 2020[137]). In Sri Lanka, the Disaster Risk Management Centre publishes risk maps, risk indices as well as inundation levels at district level although, as noted above, insurance companies have concerns about the accuracy of the available data and risk maps. In Malaysia, the Department of Irrigation and Drainage produces flood risk maps and collects data on past damages although data on flash floods is not collected (World Bank and Bank Negara Malaysia, 2024[34]). In addition, granular data and mapping has not been published due to concerns about the potential impact of this information on property prices in flood-prone areas (World Bank and Bank Negara Malaysia, 2024[34]). The Securities and Exchange Commission of Pakistan indicated that insurance companies are not leveraging the data and risk assessment tools available from disaster management and registration authorities (amongst others) and noted a lack of any large-scale data integration initiatives between insurers and public sector data providers (SECP, 2024[108]).

Insurance companies can, to some extent, address gaps in access to or availability of government data by leveraging their own claims data. However, as noted, low insurance penetration as well as evolving risks (e.g. climate change) limit the value of past claims data of individual insurers for underwriting and pricing natural hazard insurance coverage. In some countries, insurance companies (or insurance regulators) have established organisations that aggregate claims data from across the insurance sector and use the aggregated data to provide insurers with insights for use in risk assessment. In India, for example, all insurance companies are required to submit data to the Insurance Information Bureau which leverages that data as well as external sources (such as catastrophe models as well as government databases) to provide data services and analytics to the insurance sector (OECD, 2023[125]). Similarly, Insurance Services Malaysia Berhad (ISM) is an independent organisation that collects and aggregates data from its insurance and takaful member companies and external sources, and uses that data to generate risk assessment insights to support underwriting and pricing of coverage (ISM, 2020[138]). Some insurance companies in Sri Lanka noted the potential benefits of establishing a claims data sharing initiative. The Securities and Exchange Commission of Pakistan has worked to promote data sharing among insurers but has reportedly faced some industry reluctance that has limited the success of these efforts (SECP, 2024[108]).

The availability of catastrophe models is improving as the major model providers expand their offering and as technological developments allow for the entry of new players that leverage analytical tools like artificial intelligence to develop new modelling tools. Increased insurance penetration is usually positively correlated with demand for modelling tools, which drives availability. International organisations, such as the World Bank and Asian Development Bank, and initiatives such as the Global Risk Modelling Alliance have played a key role in supporting the development of models in various countries. With funding from the insurance sector and international development agencies, the Global Risk Modelling Alliance, for example, is leveraging open-source platforms to address critical model and data gaps around the world (Global Risk Modelling Alliance, 2025[139]). At the time of writing, the Alliance had active projects in eight countries across Latin America, Africa and Asia (including in Pakistan) (Global Risk Modelling Alliance, 2025[140]).

Collecting adequate premiums to underwrite risk

In order to ensure the availability of insurance coverage for natural hazard risks over the long-term, insurers must be able to charge an adequate price for the risks that they assume. If insurers are unable to charge an adequate price, whether due to regulatory or supervisory impediments or local market competitive dynamics, they are likely to turn to other approaches to managing their exposure, such as coverage exclusions, limits on sums insured or higher deductibles – or to not offer any coverage at all. As noted, the pricing of coverage for natural hazard risks in Indonesia, Malaysia, Pakistan, the Philippines and Sri Lanka is driven by a number of regulatory and market factors. Pricing guidance or requirements are imposed in Indonesia, Malaysia and the Philippines although insurers in all three countries are authorised to set premiums based on risk – and charge higher premiums for higher risk. However, in Indonesia and the Philippines, the minimum pricing requirement has become the *de facto* market price due to high-levels of price-based competition. In Malaysia, the requirement to offer the tariff product limits the ability of insurers to charge premiums above the flood tariff rate. As a result, the flood tariff rate is generally applied to pricing of flood insurance coverage. There is no applicable pricing guidance in Pakistan or Sri Lanka although both the Securities and Exchange Commission of Pakistan and the Insurance Regulatory Commission of Sri Lanka indicated that there was limited price differentiation applied to the natural hazard insurance coverage offered by insurers (although, as noted, some use by insurers of increased deductibles and exclusions to manage exposure). Price-sensitive consumers and intense competition may also limit pricing variation in Pakistan and Sri Lanka. The limited ability of some insurers to assess natural hazard risk could also limit the use of risk-based pricing (in Pakistan and Sri Lanka as well as in Indonesia, Malaysia and the Philippines).

Box 1.4. Pricing adequacy in the Philippines

Pricing for natural hazard insurance coverage is considered to be inadequate by some insurers and reinsurers in the Philippines, particularly for typhoons and floods. The non-life insurance sector, including reinsurers, have faced significant typhoon losses in recent years with loss ratios above 100% in most recent years (and sometimes significantly above 100%). Loss ratios for flood losses have also exceeded 100% in some recent years, although not by as much as typhoon losses (Figure 1.22).

In recognition of the inadequacy of the minimum (and prevailing) rates, the Insurance Commission issued a circular letter in 2022 revising the minimum rates for earthquake and typhoon/flood insurance coverage. The revised minimum rates varied depending on risk zone, occupancy and construction type, and led to rate reductions for buildings with better construction standards in low-risk zones for both earthquake and typhoon/flood coverage (to a lesser extent) along with higher minimum rates overall for typhoon/flood coverage (Insurance Commission, 2022[141]). However, stemming from several considerations, a new circular letter was issued in 2024 reinstating the previous minimum rates for both earthquake and typhoon/flood coverage (Insurance Commission, 2024[142]).

Figure 1.22. Loss ratios in fire and natural hazard insurance in the Philippines

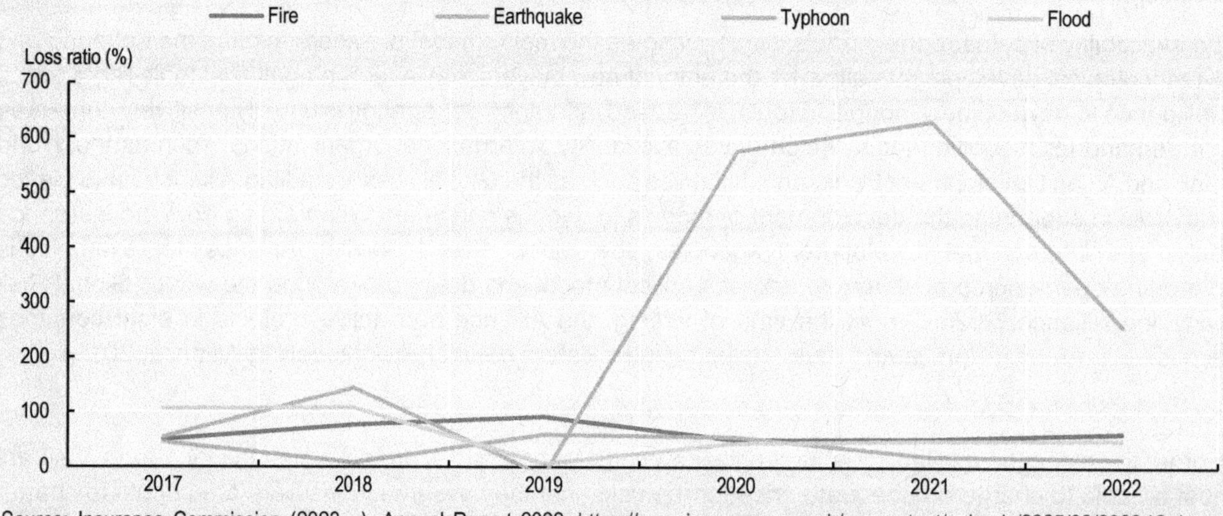

Source: Insurance Commission (2023[53]), Annual Report 2022, https://www.insurance.gov.ph/wp-content/uploads/2025/02/2022-IC-Annual-Report.pdf; Insurance Commission (2021[52]), Annual Report 2020, https://www.insurance.gov.ph/wp-content/uploads/2023/01/2020-Annual-Report-FINAL.pdf; Insurance Commission (2019[51]), Annual Report 2018, https://www.insurance.gov.ph/wp-content/uploads/2022/04/2018-Annual-Report-Final-compressed.pdf.

Limited price differentiation can lead to particular challenges if the prevailing market rate is broadly inadequate as inadequate pricing can lead insurers to limit coverage and result in higher reinsurance pricing. As mentioned, insurance and reinsurance companies in Malaysia and Pakistan indicated that pricing for natural hazard insurance coverage is generally adequate, while in Sri Lanka, pricing is mostly adequate but not high enough to attract sufficient coverage in international reinsurance markets. However, in Indonesia and the Philippines, prevailing market rates are seen by insurers and/or reinsurers as inadequate (Box 1.4).

Limited price differentiation by insurers can have other implications. Rates that do not vary with risk will not provide any risk signals or incentives for policyholder risk reduction (to the extent that policyholders have the ability to implement effective risk reduction measures) as investments to enhance resilience will not be rewarded with lower premiums. Insurance companies and/or insurance regulators in Malaysia, Pakistan, the Philippines and Sri Lanka indicated that policyholders are sometimes rewarded for taking risk reduction measures with lower premium rates, despite the limited application of risk-based pricing. However, this is likely limited to the larger corporate policyholders that are more likely to engage with insurers and intermediaries on risk management. Insurers and intermediaries, in Asia and elsewhere, do not usually provide tailored risk advice or offer substantial premium discounts for risk reduction measures to households and small businesses given the more limited amount of premiums collected from smaller policyholders (OECD, 2023[143]). Bank Negara Malaysia's Financial Sector Blueprint for 2022-2026 highlighted the potential role of digital tools in supporting climate risk adaptation, including by encouraging lower insurance premiums to reward the implementation of adaptation measures (Bank Negara Malaysia, 2022[135]). The International Association of Insurance Supervisors' recent application paper on the supervision of climate-related risks also encourages supervisors to promote risk mitigation by ensuring that insurers advertise and offer appropriate premium discounts for risk mitigation measures (IAIS, 2025[102]).

Limited price differentiation in natural hazard insurance coverage could also limit the incentives for insurance companies to make significant investment in developing risk assessment and modelling tools. Insurers will have few incentives to collect new data or apply advanced analytics if better risk assessment has no impact on pricing (OECD, 2023[125]). As a result, the insurance sector contribution to improving the availability of quality data and risk assessment tools is likely to be limited.

Insurance regulators and supervisors have a key role in overseeing the adequacy (as well as the fairness) of insurance pricing. In some cases, including in Indonesia, the Philippines and Sri Lanka, insurance supervisors review insurers' approach to pricing their coverage before providing approval for the introduction of new products. The International Association of Insurance Supervisors recently highlighted the importance of the role of supervisors in ensuring "that pricing of NatCat products reflects adequate risk-based technical models" in the context of evolving climate risks (IAIS, 2025[102]).

The capital requirements established and supervised by insurance regulators and supervisors can also have an important impact on pricing adequacy. Higher minimum capital requirements can encourage insurance sector consolidation and potentially reduce the competitive pressures that lead to intensive price competition. Minimum capital requirements have recently been increased in Indonesia, Pakistan and the Philippines. In some cases, market fragmentation and excessive competition were identified as a rationale for the capital requirement increase. The application of risk-based supervision and risk-based capital or solvency requirements should also contribute to ensuring adequate pricing. Indonesia, Malaysia, the Philippines and Sri Lanka have implemented a risk-based capital framework (Norton Rose Fulbright, 2024[134]). The Securities and Exchange Commission of Pakistan intends to implement risk-based capital requirements by 2027 (SECP, 2024[103]).

Given the complexity of assessing and quantifying natural hazard risks, supervisors in Asia and elsewhere will likely face difficulties in overseeing pricing adequacy through product approval and risk-based supervision and capital requirements. Assessing pricing adequacy and pricing-related risks requires supervisory resources with sufficient actuarial and modelling expertise – which can be challenging in countries with a limited pool of qualified actuaries and modellers. Insurance regulators and supervisors in a number of the countries that contributed to this report identified a lack of actuarial and/or modelling expertise as a significant challenge.

In recognition of the increasing risk posed by natural hazards, the complexity of risk assessment in a changing climate and the growing use of sophisticated catastrophe models, insurance supervisors in Europe and the United States are investing additional resources to help build supervisory expertise in catastrophe modelling. The European Insurance and Occupational Pensions Authority has established a centre of excellence for catastrophe modelling and data aimed at providing European supervisors and insurers with expertise, data and tools to support risk assessment and the supervision of natural hazard risks (EIOPA, n.d.[144]). In the United States, the National Association of Insurance Commissioners has established a Catastrophe Modeling Center of Excellence to provide regulators with technical training and expertise on catastrophe models and to apply catastrophe models in assessing the risk of losses from natural hazards (NAIC, n.d.[145]).

Sustainable access to affordable reinsurance

Access to affordable reinsurance coverage is critical for ensuring the availability of affordable insurance coverage for natural hazard risks for households and businesses. Some insurers in Malaysia, Pakistan, the Philippines - and particularly in Indonesia and Sri Lanka - have faced challenges in accessing affordable reinsurance coverage due to the quality of data on insured exposures and adequacy of premium pricing.

Reinsurance companies as well as intermediaries often play a critical role in providing access to data and risk assessment tools. International reinsurance companies often develop their own models or acquire licenses to models from other providers and have dedicated modelling teams to support their approach to assuming and pricing risk from insurers. They also play an important role in supporting pricing adequacy. In the case of proportional placements, they can encourage pricing adequacy by setting pricing conditions as a prerequisite to assuming risk. In the case of non-proportional placements, reinsurers may increase insurer retentions (i.e. insurer deductibles) as a means to encourage insurers to improve pricing adequacy.

Regulatory restrictions on access to international markets could have an impact on the contribution that international reinsurers make to risk assessment and pricing adequacy. While preferential placements with national reinsurers and some limitations on cross-border risk transfer exist in Indonesia, Malaysia, Pakistan, the Philippines and Sri Lanka, international reinsurers are nonetheless significant participants in assuming risk from all of these countries and broadly contribute to risk assessment and pricing adequacy.

The national reinsurers in Indonesia and Malaysia have also supported insurance sector access to data and tools. For example, Malaysia Re developed an in-house flood model and provided access to the model to its insurance consumers (although the model is no longer in use). Indonesia Re operates the National Insurance Data Center Management Agency (BPPDAN) which provides annual statistics on loss experience by occupation based on data collected from across the insurance sector (Indonesia Re, 2025[146]). Maipark, which is an industry-owned reinsurer for earthquake and others natural hazard risks in Indonesia, has developed a probabilistic earthquake risk model and is working on expanding it to incorporate flood and other climate-related risks. Maipark also provides training to insurance companies on how to apply its modelling tools.

The national reinsurers in Indonesia and the Philippines have also contributed to pricing discipline. After facing significant losses in recent years, Indonesia Re and the other Indonesian reinsurers have increased pricing for non-proportional placements and imposed higher retentions on both proportional and non-proportional placements in order to improve the ceding insurers' incentives to ensure pricing adequacy (given the increased exposure that insurers will need to retain). In the Philippines, Nat Re is imposing compliance with the minimum tariff pricing by excluding non-compliant policies from treaty placements.

National reinsurers play different roles in providing reinsurance capacity to the domestic insurance market. The national reinsurers in Indonesia, Malaysia and the Philippines tend to be significant capacity providers and are often offered a greater share of placements than required by the preferential system. The national reinsurers in Pakistan and Sri Lanka face more capacity constraints and are not generally offered more than required. They also play different roles for different types of insurers. The national reinsurers in the Philippines and Pakistan, for example, tend to be a more important capacity provider for smaller insurers. However, as noted above, none of the national reinsurers are able to play a countercyclical role during hard reinsurance markets given the (syndicated) nature of reinsurance placements and their reliance on retrocession to international markets.

The differences in national reinsurer capacity and market impact are driven by a number of factors. The National Insurance Trust Fund in Sri Lanka is a wholly owned government agency and is perceived by insurers as operating like a government department rather than a private sector reinsurance company. Insurers in Pakistan have a similar perception of the Pakistan Reinsurance Company, even though the company is partially listed. The two wholly owned national reinsurers in Indonesia, on the other hand, are generally perceived as professional reinsurance companies.

The national reinsurers also have different capacities for assuming risk from outside their home jurisdiction, and therefore differing abilities to establish an internationally diversified portfolio of risks. Malaysia Re has assumed significant risk from outside Malaysia (more than 50% of its portfolio) and can compete based on its high credit rating (which is higher than Malaysia's sovereign rating). Nat Re also assumes business outside of the Philippines although not to the same extent as Malaysia Re. The government-owned national reinsurers in Indonesia have more difficulty competing for international business as they have not been provided with sufficient capital from the Indonesian government to achieve the necessary credit rating. The National Insurance Trust Fund in Sri Lanka and the Pakistan Reinsurance Company do not assume international business and do not have independent credit ratings.[36] As noted above, the lack of international diversification creates concentration risk for those national reinsurers and can ultimately lead to counterparty risks for domestic insurers that have ceded significant risk to those national reinsurers.

Ultimately, policy makers should aim to find a sustainable balance that supports long-term access to affordable reinsurance capacity. Improved access to international reinsurance and capital markets (Box 1.5) can help ensure that capacity is available to absorb the expected increase in natural hazard losses. International reinsurance markets allow for losses to be diversified away from the domestic financial system and have likely reduced the economic disruption caused by past significant events (OECD, 2018[45]).[37]

Box 1.5. Risk transfer to capital markets

Through insurance-linked securities and other alternative reinsurance structures, insurers and reinsurers around the world have increasingly transferred natural hazard risks directly to capital markets. According to one estimate, the annual issuance of catastrophe bonds and other insurance-linked securities has increased from approximately USD 1.4 billion annually between 2000 and 2004 to more than USD 14.1 billion annually between 2020 and 2024 (Artemis, n.d.[147]). The development of the insurance-linked securities market has provided an additional source of reinsurance capacity for natural hazard risks and has likely dampened the impact of cyclical reinsurance pricing (OECD, 2018[45]).

In some countries, regulators may not allow supervised insurers to transfer risk to capital markets or may not allow insurers to recognise such transfers as effective reinsurance arrangements that warrant a corresponding reduction in reserve and capital requirements (OECD, 2020[148]). Insurance companies and/or regulators in Malaysia, Pakistan, the Philippines and Sri Lanka did not identify any limitations on the use or recognition of risk transfer to capital markets, although some insurers in Indonesia indicated that risk transfer to capital markets is not permitted.[1] The Securities and Exchange Commission of Pakistan has indicated an interest in increasing insurance-linked securities market capacity to assume risk from insurers in Pakistan (SECP, 2024[103]).

Figure 1.23. Catastrophe bond and insurance-liked securities outstanding for natural hazard perils

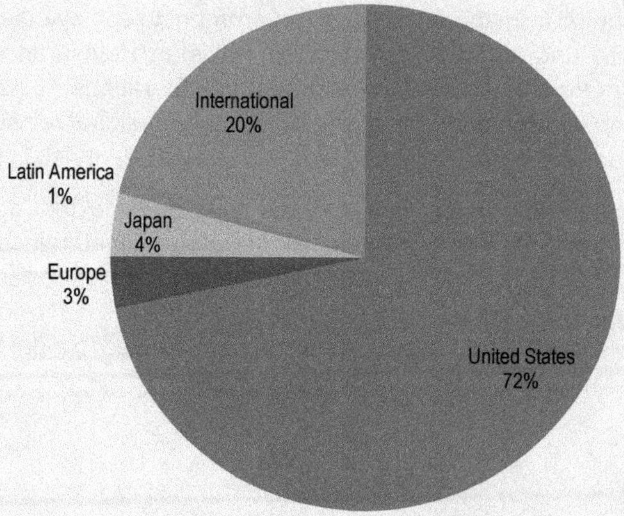

Note: 1. An OECD examination of the regulatory framework for reinsurance in Asian countries in 2020 identified some limitations in the recognition of risk transfer to capital markets in Indonesia and the Philippines (OECD, 2020[148]).
Source: OECD calculations based on data provided by Artemis (n.d.[149])

However, there has been very limited issuance of capital bonds and other insurance-linked securities to provide financial protection against natural hazard risks in Asia (outside of Japan) (Figure 1.23). There have been a number of efforts to expand this market in Asia, including the development of tailored licensing and regulatory frameworks for catastrophe bond issuance in Singapore and Hong Kong (China) (OECD, 2020[148]).

National reinsurers can make an important contribution to supporting that access by addressing gaps in capacity and promoting efforts to improve data quality and pricing adequacy among domestic insurers. National reinsurers receive a benefit through their preferential access to domestic reinsurance placements and should therefore be required to contribute to building sustainable access to affordable reinsurance.

Establishing public private insurance programmes

Public-private insurance programmes (PPIPs), also referred to as catastrophe risk insurance programmes, are arrangements established by the insurance sector and/or government to provide insurance, co-insurance, reinsurance and/or a government guarantee for losses resulting from natural hazards or other types of catastrophe perils to households and businesses (OECD, 2021[150]). These arrangements may be established by the private insurance sector, such as through the creation of a co-insurance pool among insurers or a reinsurer owned by the insurance sector. They could also be established by the public sector as a state-owned insurer or reinsurer.

In the context of increasing losses and challenges in the availability and affordability of private insurance coverage, an increasing number of OECD countries have established public-private insurance programmes in recent years.[38] These programmes have taken various forms, including government-owned direct insurers or compensation programmes (e.g. Denmark, Iceland, New Zealand, Spain, Switzerland[39], the United States[40]) and government-owned reinsurers (Australia, France, Japan, the United States[41]), as well as private sector co-insurance pools (Belgium, Norway, Switzerland[40]) and special-purpose insurers and reinsurers (Republic of Türkiye (hereafter "Türkiye"), the United Kingdom). Recognising the potential need for these types of arrangements, the G7 Finance Ministers and Central Bank Governors welcomed a *High-Level Framework for Public-Private Insurance Programmes against Natural Hazards* at their meeting in May 2024, developed by the G7 Climate Change Mitigation Working Group with input from the OECD and the International Association of Insurance Supervisors (G7 Finance Track, 2024[151]). The High-Level Framework provides a set of considerations for the establishment of public-private insurance programmes to address protection gaps for natural hazard risks, including possible objectives and design features.

Public-private insurance programmes can contribute to addressing protection gaps for natural hazard risks by: (i) pooling the risks of many policyholders in order to achieve a more diversified pool of risks that reduces the potential that a large share of the pool's covered policyholders are affected by losses simultaneously and the corresponding amount of capital and reserves that would need to be set-aside, which can support affordability; (ii) limiting the potential magnitude of losses that individual insurers or reinsurers could face, with similar benefits in terms of capital and reserve needs and affordability; and (iii) improving the availability of data and modelling of natural hazard risks (OECD, 2021[150]). The OECD countries that have established public-private insurance programmes tend to have achieved higher levels of insurance coverage of natural hazard losses and have faced fewer protection gaps (Figure 1.24).

Figure 1.24. The impact of PPIPs on flood insurance protection gaps

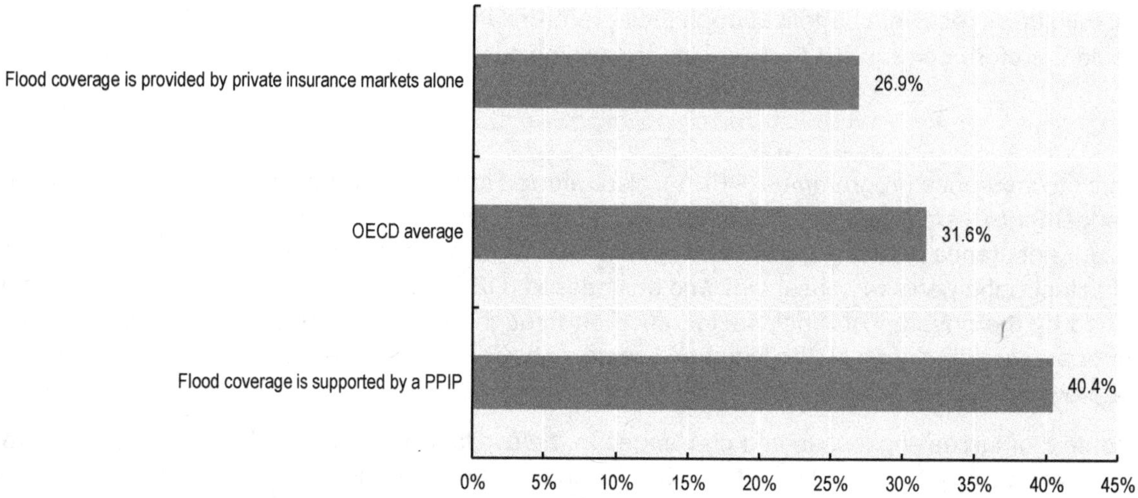

Source: OECD calculations based on data provided by Swiss Re (Swiss Re, sigma database. All rights reserved.).

The establishment of public-private insurance programmes to support coverage for natural hazard risks to households and businesses has been less common in Asia, and in emerging and developing countries more generally.[41] A few programmes have been established in emerging and developing countries, including in Algeria, Morocco, Romania and (as noted above) Türkiye:

- In Algeria, households and businesses are required to acquire a "CatNat" coverage for natural hazard risks with reinsurance available from a government reinsurer (*Compagnie Centrale de Réassurance*). The programme covers earthquakes, floods, landslides, mudslides and storm and violent winds.
- In Morocco, property insurance coverage for households and businesses is automatically extended to include coverage for natural hazard risks (floods, mudslides, earthquakes and tsunamis) and assumed by an industry co-insurance pool.
- In Romania, a special-purpose insurance company (*Pool-ul de Asigurare Împotriva Dezastrelor Naturale (PAID)*) has been established to provide basic coverage for households for losses from earthquakes and floods. The stand-alone coverage is mandatory for all households.
- In Türkiye, a public insurer (*Doğal Afet Sigortaları Kurumu* or Turkish Catastrophe Insurance Pool) has been established to provide basic coverage for households and some businesses against losses from earthquakes and from fires, tsunamis or landslides caused by earthquakes. The stand-alone coverage is mandatory for households (and some businesses) in urban areas. There are plans to extend the programme to include other natural hazard risks.

A public-private insurance programme has also been established in Indonesia for earthquake and related risks (i.e. the natural hazards included in the EQVET (earthquake, volcanic eruption and tsunami) coverage offered by insurers). Maipark is a reinsurance company owned by all non-life insurance companies that provides reinsurance to Indonesian insurers for the EQVET coverage provided to households and businesses.[42] All Indonesian non-life insurers cede a minimum amount of this risk to Maipark (10% for the island of Java and 25% elsewhere) on a compulsory basis with the possibility of ceding a greater amount. As noted above, Maipark also plays a critical role in supporting the availability of data and modelling on earthquake and other natural hazard risks.

There have also been efforts to establish a programme in the Philippines. The insurance industry, the national reinsurer (Nat Re) and the Insurance Commission collaborated to establish the Philippine

Catastrophe Insurance Facility (PCIF) as a voluntary[43] co-insurance and reinsurance arrangement for natural hazard risks, with the aim of expanding the take-up of coverage for natural hazard risks on a sustainable basis. The pool would assume up to 25% of the natural hazard risk underwritten by participating insurance companies and retrocede a share to member insurers, Nat Re and international markets. Given the need to ensure pricing adequacy within the PCIF, a working group undertook modelling of natural hazard risks with the aim of updating the pricing framework for natural hazard risks, culminating in the new pricing framework proposed in 2022 (Insurance Commission, 2022[141]) which was revoked in 2024 (Insurance Commission, 2024[142]). The reinstatement of the previous minimum tariffs has delayed the implementation of the PCIF although the members have reportedly agreed to proceed with the arrangement for earthquake coverage given that the pricing is deemed to be more adequate for this risk.

Sri Lanka established a programme through the National Insurance Trust Fund, a government agency and national reinsurer, that focused on providing coverage for uninsured households and small businesses, but it is no longer in operation. The National Natural Disaster Insurance Policy provided coverage between 2016 and 2018 for damages from cyclones, storms, floods, landslides, earthquakes, tsunamis and other natural hazard perils. The programme was backed by a specific reinsurance policy and incorporated a ceiling on payments per event and per year, calibrated to the acquired reinsurance policy. However, major flooding in Colombo in 2016 and other factors led to an increase in the cost of reinsurance coverage that eventually led to the termination of the programme. Insurance companies in Sri Lanka have proposed the need for a new programme to provide basic and affordable coverage through some form of pooling arrangement with government backing.

The Securities and Exchange Commission of Pakistan is interested in facilitating the creation of an insurance pool (SECP, 2024[103]) and developed a report examining international approaches and potential models for such a pool in Pakistan (SECP, 2024[136]). The report considers three possible structural approaches to pooling (voluntary co-insurance arrangement, a separate legal entity and a statutory body) and the possibility of including agricultural risks, motor third party liability as well as natural hazard risks (SECP, 2024[136]).

Bank Negara Malaysia's Financial Sector Blueprint for 2022-2026 similarly includes a commitment to explore the possible establishment of public-private risk pools to deal with high-risk, large-scale perils, including climate-related natural hazards as well as pandemics, cyber risk and environmental risks (Bank Negara Malaysia, 2022[135]). A possible approach identified for consideration would involve a first-loss coverage from the private insurance and takaful sector with potential public sector support for initial capacity development and backstops. As noted above, some Malaysian insurers have proposed the inclusion of basic, first-loss flood insurance coverage on an opt-out basis, which would be consistent with the approach outlined in the Financial Sector Blueprint. The World Bank has also recommended a compulsory basic coverage as a means to address challenges to the availability of flood insurance coverage for high-risk SMEs (World Bank and Bank Negara Malaysia, 2024[34]).

The establishment of public-private insurance programmes in emerging markets and developing countries needs to consider several factors. These include: (i) the government's policy objectives in terms of who should be protected; (ii) the level of insurance market development (and financial sector development more broadly); and (iii) the financial and institutional capacity of the government to prepare for and respond to disasters (Adam, Hallegate and Mahul, 2025[152]). In the case of programmes that target households and businesses in developing countries with higher levels of insurance and financial market development, the note proposes an approach that leverages domestic insurance market and international reinsurance market capacity, provides premium subsidies to households and micro and small business, and incorporates a contribution from governments as reinsurers of last resort (Adam, Hallegate and Mahul, 2025[152]).

The established public-private insurance programmes take a broad range of approaches to leveraging private (re)insurance market capacity and incorporating public financial support. Some programmes act as residual programmes focused on high-risk households, and possibly businesses, and transfer significant risk to private reinsurance or retrocession markets (e.g. Flood Re in the United Kingdom) while others are the main providers of insurance coverage for natural hazard risks and retain most of the risk that they assume (e.g. *Consorcio de Compensación de Seguros* in Spain). Very few of the existing models incorporate explicit premium subsidies although many provide implicit subsidies and/or cross-subsidies by incorporating minimal risk variation in pricing or by ensuring that pricing is affordable, even if that leads to more frequent losses for the government as backstop provider.

The existing programmes in emerging and developing countries have tended to be the main providers of coverage for natural hazard risks in the countries where they operate (rather than residual providers), although all of these programmes transfer significant risk to international reinsurance markets. The programmes in Romania and Türkiye provide only basic (first-loss) coverage which could be supplemented by private insurance for residual natural hazard losses although the market for private (supplemental) insurance is limited in both countries and a significant share of losses have remained uninsured.

Premiums for natural hazard insurance coverage in Algeria, Morocco and Romania are not significantly risk-based and therefore entail some cross-subsidies. Premiums for earthquake coverage in Türkiye incorporate some risk factors and the proposed approach to premium pricing for other hazards will reportedly be risk-based. There are no explicit premium subsidies incorporated into any of these programmes. However, cross-subsidisation between low- and high-risk policyholders, as well as the limits on sum insured in Romania and Türkiye, help ensure affordability – which is critical for programmes that impose mandatory purchase requirements. The programme in Morocco incorporates an innovative feature to support more vulnerable segments of the population that are unlikely to be insured. A small premium tax is added to natural hazard coverage to create a solidarity fund that makes compensation payments to uninsured households impacted by natural hazards. As noted above, the discontinued National Natural Disaster Insurance Policy in Sri Lanka similarly focused on providing support to those unable to acquire insurance coverage. The Philippine Catastrophe Insurance Facility is also considering the incorporation of a limited (microinsurance) coverage for households and micro and small businesses.

The level of government reinsurance or backstop support also tends to be more limited for the programmes in emerging and developing countries (relative to the support provided in developed countries). The programme in Türkiye has access to an "Excess-of-Loss" arrangement with the government if it has not been able to secure sufficient financial protection in private reinsurance markets (DASK, 2012[153]) while the programme in Romania has access to repayable government loans if needed. An inability to access government support could have implications for the programme's ability to provide significant capacity. For example, Maipark in Indonesia does not benefit from a government reinsurance coverage or backstop and may face capacity constraints in the future if it is unable to raise sufficient capital from its shareholders to meet higher capital requirements (as its insurance company shareholders also face an increase in capital requirements).

1.4. Conclusion

Emerging and developing Asia and Pacific countries face significant protection gaps in natural hazard insurance, which leave households and businesses unprotected against damages and losses from natural hazards and could create burdens on public finances and potential risks to financial stability. Economic losses from natural hazards are increasing across the region, driven in part by the impacts of changes in hazard frequency and intensity. The increasing losses could lead to an increase in the cost of insurance that will make it increasingly difficult to close protection gaps for natural hazard risks.

This chapter examined the drivers of protection gaps in Asia focusing on the experiences of Indonesia, Malaysia, Pakistan, the Philippines and Sri Lanka. Protection gaps in natural hazard insurance result from factors that limit the demand for insurance coverage and reduce the willingness of households and businesses to pay for insurance coverage, as well as factors that impact the supply of insurance coverage which can limit the availability and affordability of insurance coverage for these risks.

There appears to be a high level of risk awareness and perception of natural hazards in many parts of Asia relative to other parts of the world given their frequency. However, the relatively high level of natural hazard risk perception does not translate to broad take-up of insurance coverage. This is likely due to a limited understanding of the need for and benefits of insurance coverage to protect against these risks and a lack of trust in insurance as an effective form of financial protection. Differences in insurers' approach to offering natural hazard insurance coverage may also be leading to misunderstandings about the availability of coverage and the need, in some cases, to acquire specific additional coverage. For lower-income segments of the population and those in high-risk areas, insurance coverage may simply be unaffordable given other more urgent expenditure needs.

Limited access to quality data and risk assessment tools such as catastrophe models can lead insurers to limit the coverage they make available to households and businesses. It can also inhibit their ability to price premiums based on risk, although intensive competition and price-sensitive consumers discourages insurers from charging higher premiums in higher risk areas. As a result, insurers tend to impose higher deductibles, limit the sums insured or exclude coverage for some or all natural hazard risks, rather than charge higher premiums. The challenges in quantifying natural hazard risks, along with concerns about premium pricing adequacy in some countries, have led to some difficulties in accessing affordable reinsurance coverage, particularly proportional coverage. A lack of access to affordable reinsurance reduces the appetite of insurers for providing coverage for natural hazard risks to households and businesses.

Translating the relatively high-level of risk awareness into broader levels of financial protection for natural hazard risks will require further investment across a number of areas, including:

- Improving insurance literacy, with a focus on building understanding of the benefits of, and need for, insurance coverage against natural hazard risks.
- Increasing trust in insurance companies and insurance coverage as an effective form of financial protection, including through efforts to improve awareness of the role of insurance supervisors in protecting consumers and, where applicable, the protection provided through policyholder protection schemes.
- Augmenting property insurance penetration by: (i) enhancing the use of digital distribution channels and bancassurance, leveraging increased access to banks and digital technologies; and (ii) encouraging the development of suitable and affordable insurance coverage products, including microinsurance, parametric and takaful and sharia products, and providing flexibilities that support the attractiveness and reach of these products.
- Expanding the take-up of natural hazard coverage by encouraging insurers to implement consistent approaches in how they offer this coverage and improve clarity on coverage and exclusions, and by considering the potential advantages (and disadvantages) of requiring insurers to offer natural hazard coverage (or basic natural hazard coverage) automatically in property insurance coverage.

Ensuring the availability of insurance coverage for natural hazard risks will require:

- Efforts to improve access to quality data and modelling tools, including by improving the quality of – and access to – government data on hazards and exposures, examining the establishment of claims data sharing initiatives within the insurance sector and leveraging opportunities to access international assistance for model development.
- Improving the ability of insurers to adequately price coverage for natural hazard insurance and provide pricing incentives for risk reduction, as well as the capacity of insurance supervisors to oversee pricing adequacy, including by building expertise in the use of catastrophe models and other sophisticated risk assessment tools.

- Supporting sustainable access to affordable reinsurance capacity, including through capital markets, by addressing the factors that impede access (data quality, pricing adequacy) and enhancing the contribution of national reinsurers to addressing gaps in capacity, including retakaful capacity.

Public-private insurance programmes can make an important contribution to ensuring the availability of affordable insurance coverage for natural hazard risks. The design of such programmes should take into account local factors, such as the level of insurance market development and the capacity of governments to share some of the risk. Responding to the needs of vulnerable segments of the population should be a key objective in the design of such programmes.

The challenges outlined in this chapter to increasing demand for natural hazard insurance coverage and enhancing the insurance sector's capacity to assume natural hazard risks are shared by countries around the world. As a result, there are significant opportunities to share experience and learn from the efforts of other countries to address these challenges.

References

AAUI (2018), *Vision and mission*, Asosiasi Asuransi Umum Indonesia. [75]

Abbas, A. et al. (2015), "Non-structural flood risk mitigation under developing country conditions: an analysis on the determinants of willingness to pay for flood insurance in rural Pakistan", *Natural Hazards*, Vol. 75/3, pp. 2119-2135, https://doi.org/10.1007/S11069-014-1415-X/TABLES/4. [157]

Ada derana Business (2019), "Boosting the Insurance industry and the role of the MSF", *Ada derana Business*. [79]

Adam, B., S. Hallegate and O. Mahul (2025), *Mobilizing public-private solutions to manage the financial impacts of natural hazards in emerging markets and developing economies: Challenges and opportunities of operationalizing Public-Private Insurance Programs*, World Bank. [152]

ADB (2024), *Asia-Pacific Climate Report 2024*, Asian Development Bank, Manila, Philippines, https://doi.org/10.22617/SGP240498-2. [3]

Adhi, I. et al. (2019), "The Right to Live Dangerously: Public Perceptions of Extreme Water Events in Urban Areas", pp. 29-36, https://doi.org/10.2991/ICSGS-18.2019.5. [16]

Allen, T. et al. (2023), "Climate change and residential real estate: what are the risks for the banking sector?", *Bulletin*, Banque de France. [99]

Aon (2024), *Navigating Catastrophe Risk: Model Coverage, ELEMENTS 18.* [35]

Artemis (2025), *Guy Carpenter Global Property Catastrophe Rate-On-Line Index*, Artemis. [63]

Artemis (2025), *Guy Carpenter Regional Property Catastrophe Rate-On-Line Index*, Artemis. [64]

Artemis (n.d.), *Catastrophe bonds & ILS issued and outstanding by year*, Artemis. [147]

Artemis (n.d.), *Catastrophe bonds & ILS outstanding by risk or peril*, Artemis. [149]

ASEAN Insurance Council (2023), *Comparison Among Countries in ASEAN with Existing Insurance Policy Guarantee Scheme*. [87]

Asia Insurance Review (2023), “Deposit Insurance Corporation gets ready to implement Policy Guarantee Programme”, *Asia Insurance Review*. [88]

Asian Development Bank (2024), *The Enabling Environment for Disaster Risk Financing in the Philippines*, Asian Development Bank, Manila, Philippines, https://doi.org/10.22617/TCS240611-2. [119]

Ayyagari, M. and T. Beck (2015), “Financial Inclusion in Asia: An Overview”, *Economics Working Papers*, Asian Development Bank. [165]

Bank Negara Malaysia (2025), *Financial Consumer Alert List*, Bank Negara Malaysia. [82]

Bank Negara Malaysia (2024), *General Insurance: Distribution of Gross Direct Premiums*, Bank Negara Malaysia. [130]

Bank Negara Malaysia (2024), *General Takaful: Distribution of Gross Contributions of Direct Takaful Operators*, Bank Negara Malaysia. [131]

Bank Negara Malaysia (2024), *Policy Document on Licensing and Regulatory Framework for Digital Insurers and Takaful Operators*, Bank Negara Malaysia. [110]

Bank Negara Malaysia (2022), *Financial Sector Blueprint: 2022-2026*, Bank Negara Malaysia. [135]

Bank Negara Malaysia (2021), *Perlindungan Tenang*, Bank Negara Malaysia. [123]

Bank Negara Malaysia (2019), *Takaful Operational Framework*, Bank Negara Malaysia. [132]

Bank of England (2019), *Climate change: what are the risks to financial stability?*, Bank of England. [100]

Biese, K. et al. (2023), *Inclusive insurance and risk financing in Indonesia: Snapshot and way forward 2023*, United Nations Development Programme. [113]

Bronfman, N. et al. (2020), “Understanding the Relationship Between Direct Experience and Risk Perception of Natural Hazards”, *Risk Analysis*, Vol. 40/10, pp. 2057-2070, https://doi.org/10.1111/RISA.13526. [11]

Brown, J. and A. Goolsbee (2000), “Does the Internet Make Markets More Competitive? Evidence from the Life Insurance Industry”, *SSRN Electronic Journal*, https://doi.org/10.2139/ssrn.253795. [111]

Bündnis Entwicklung Hilft and IFHV (2024), *World Risk Report*, Bündnis Entwicklung Hilft. [170]

CATRisk Solutions (n.d.), *CATRisk Geographic Model Coverage*, CATRisk Solutions. [41]

Central Bank of Sri Lanka (2024), *Financial Literacy Roadmap of Sri Lanka (2024 - 2028)*, Central Bank of Sri Lanka. [70]

Central Bank of Sri Lanka (2021), *National Financial Inclusion Strategy: 2021-2024*, Central Bank of Sri Lanka. [69]

Centre for Research on the Epidemiology of Disasters (CRED) (n.d.), *EM-DAT*. [20]

Chanel, S. and R. Singh (2025), "UN, Samoa Surety Insurance to unveil "transformative" climate solution", *Samoa Observer*. [120]

Chen, C. et al. (2025), *Vulnerability (2022)*, University of Notre Dame Global Adaptation Initiative. [171]

Chen, C. et al. (2025), *Exposure (2022)*, University of Notre Dame Global Adaptation Initiative. [2]

Cisternas, P. et al. (2024), "The influence of risk awareness and government trust on risk perception and preparedness for natural hazards", *Risk Analysis*, Vol. 44/2, pp. 333-348, https://doi.org/10.1111/RISA.14151. [9]

COMBUS (n.d.), *Models*, COMBUS Pty. [43]

Comisión para el Mercado Financiero (2024), *CMF publishes for consultation regulation on parametric insurance*, Comisión para el Mercado Financiero. [127]

Courbage, C. and C. Nicolas (2019), "Who Trusts Insurance? Empirical Evidence from Seven Industrialised Countries", *SSRN Electronic Journal*, https://doi.org/10.2139/SSRN.3404821. [27]

DASK (2012), *Law*, Doğal Afet Sigortaları Kurumu. [153]

Department of Statistics Malaysia (2022), *Household Income by Percentile*, Department of Statistics Malaysia. [30]

EIOPA (2024), *Measures to address demand side aspects of the NatCat protection gap*, European Insurance and Occupational Pensions Authority. [4]

EIOPA (2019), *Consultation Paper on Proposals for Solvency II 2020 Review Harmonisation of National Insurance Guarantee Schemes*, EIOPA. [89]

EIOPA (n.d.), *Centre of excellence for catastrophe modelling and data*, European Insurance and Occupational Pensions Authority. [144]

Esho, N. et al. (2004), "Law and the Determinants of Property-Casualty Insurance", *The Journal of Risk and Insurance*, Vol. 71/2. [92]

European Central Bank and European Systemic Risk Board (2023), *Towards macroprudential frameworks for managing climate risk*, European Systemic Risk Board. [98]

Everett-Allen, K. (2022), *Which countries have the highest proportion of mortgage-free households?*, Knight Frank. [160]

Financial Education Network (2025), *Discussion Paper on the Proposed Features of Malaysia's Second National Strategy for Financial Literacy (2026 – 2030)*, Bank Negara Malaysia. [71]

Financial Inclusion Steering Committee (2024), *2023 Annual Report: National Strategy for Financial Inclusion*, Financial Inclusion Steering Committee. [72]

G7 Finance Track (2024), *High-Level Framework for Public-Private Insurance Programmes against Natural Hazards*. [151]

Gallagher, J. (2014), "Learning about an Infrequent Event: Evidence from Flood Insurance Take-Up in the United States", *American Economic Journal: Applied Economics*, Vol. 6/3, pp. 206-233, https://doi.org/10.1257/app.6.3.206. [14]

Garcia Ocampo, D. and C. Lopez Moreira (2024), "Uncertain waters: can parametric insurance help bridge NatCat protection gaps?", *FSI Insights on policy implementation*, No. 62, Bank for International Settlements. [126]

Global Market Insights (2025), *Parametric Insurance Market Size - By Coverage, By Distribution Channel, By Application, By End Use, Analysis, Share, Growth Forecast, 2025 - 2034*, Global Market Insights. [124]

Global Risk Modelling Alliance (2025), *About the Alliance*, Global Risk Modelling Alliance. [139]

Global Risk Modelling Alliance (2025), *Country map*, Global Risk Modelling Alliance. [140]

Government of Indonesia (2023), *Undang-undang (UU) Nomor 4 Tahun 2023 tentang Pengembangan dan Penguatan Sektor Keuangan*, Database Peraturan. [94]

Guy Carpenter (2025), *January 1, 2025 Reinsurance Renwal*, Guy Carpenter. [46]

Guy Carpenter (2024), *APAC Property Catastrophe Rate on Line Index*. [62]

Guy Carpenter (2024), *Global Property Catastrophe Rate on Line Index*. [61]

Guy Carpenter (2024), *Strong reinsurer appetite drives excess property catastrophe capacity at January 1*, Guy Carpenter. [60]

Hassan, H. and S. Abbas (2019), "Factors influencing the investors' intention to adopt Takaful (Islamic insurance) products: A survey of Pakistan", *Journal of Islamic Marketing*, Vol. 11/1. [28]

Helgi Library (2025), *Mortgage Loans (as % of GDP)*, Helgi Library. [159]

Helgi Library (2025), *Mortgage Loans (As % of GDP) in Indonesia*, Helgi Library. [162]

Helgi Library (2025), *Mortgage Loans (As % of GDP) in Malaysia*, Helgi Library. [163]

Helgi Library (2025), *Mortgage Loans (As % of GDP) in Philippines*, Helgi Library. [161]

Hoque, M., S. Hossain and M. Siddique (2023), "Financial Inclusion and its Determinants: Empirical Evidence from South Asia", *The Journal of Developing Areas*, Vol. 57/3, pp. 199-211, https://doi.org/10.1353/JDA.2023.A907742. [167]

IAIS (2025), *Application Paper on the supervision of climate-related risks in the insurance sector*, International Association of Insurance Supervisors. [102]

IAIS (2023), *Issues Paper on Insurance Sector Operational Resilience*, International Association of Insurance Supervisors. [177]

IAIS (2023), *Issues Paper on roles and functioning of policyholder protection schemes (PPSs)*, International Association of Insurance Supervisors. [83]

IMF (2024), *World Economic Outlook Database, October 2024*, International Monetary Fund. [91]

Indonesia Re (2025), *History of BPPDAN*, Indonesia Re. [146]

Ingram, A. (2025), *Is Bancassurance Poised to Lead the SME Commercial Insurance Market?*, Sapiens. [107]

Insurance Asia (2025), "Micro insurance market to grow 6.5% annually until 2032", *Insurance Asia*. [175]

Insurance Asia (2025), "Microinsurance expands to cover 344m globally in 2024", *Insurance Asia*. [117]

Insurance Association of Pakistan (n.d.), *About IAP*, Insurance Association of Pakistan. [77]

Insurance Association of Pakistan (n.d.), *Insurance & Takaful Day*, Insurance Association of Pakistan. [174]

Insurance Board of Sri Lanka (2019), *Know more about Insurance*, Insurance Regulatory Commission of Sri Lanka. [74]

Insurance Commission (2025), *Guidelines on Inclusive Micro Products*, Insurance Commission. [122]

Insurance Commission (2024), *Circular Letter No. 2024-13 | Consolidated Guidelines for Takaful Window Operation*, Insurance Commission. [133]

Insurance Commission (2024), *Reinstatement of Circular Letter No. 2016-55 on the "Strict Implementation of the Minimum Rates for Earthquake, Typhoon and Flood Covers and Related Guidelines" and Participation in the Philippine Catastrophe Insurance Facility (PCIF)*, Insurance Commission. [142]

Insurance Commission (2023), *Annual Report 2022*, Insurance Commission. [53]

Insurance Commission (2022), *Guidelines on the Adoption of the Revised Schedule of Minimum Catastrophe Rates*, Insurance Commission. [141]

Insurance Commission (2021), *Annual Report 2020*, Insurance Commission. [52]

Insurance Commission (2020), *Dissemination of Information on the Georisk Philippines Initiative as an Underwriting Tool for Non-LIfe Insurance Companies*, Insurance Commission. [137]

Insurance Commission (2019), *Annual Report 2018*, Insurance Commission. [51]

Insurance Commission (2017), *Annual Report 2016*, Insurance Commission. [50]

Insurance Commission (2015), *Annual Report 2014*, Insurance Commission. [49]

Insurance Commission (n.d.), *A Glimpse of Microinsurance in the Philippines (Primer)*. [121]

Insurance Development Forum (2025), *CatRiskTools*, Insurance Development Forum. [44]

Insurance Journal (2024), "Survey: Most Homeowners Believe Their Policy Covers Flood", *Insurance Journal*. [23]

IRCSL (2024), *Industry Handbook 2023*, Insurance Regulatory Commission of Sri Lanka. [59]

IRCSL (2022), *Statistical Review 2021*, Insurance Regulatory Commission of Sri Lanka. [58]

IRCSL (2020), *Statistical Review 2019*, Insurance Regulatory Commission of Sri Lanka. [57]

IRCSL (2018), *Statistical Review 2017*, Insurance Regulatory Commission of Sri Lanka. [56]

IRCSL and University of Colombo (2024), *Public Confidence in Insurance in Sri Lanka*. [26]

ISM (2020), *About Us*, Insurance Services Malaysia Berhad. [138]

Ismail, F., N. Sivarajah and Q. Chow (2020), *Asia Microinsurance Supply-side Study*, MicroInsurance Centre at Milliman. [115]

ITMinds Limited (2025), *Why Emlaak Financials*, Emlaak Financials. [112]

Jama Punji (2017), *Insurance - Your Protection Against Risk: A Concise Guide*, Securities and Exchange Commission of Pakistan. [73]

Kahn, C., A. Panjwani and J. Santos (2024), "Insurance, Weather, and Financial Stability", *Finance and Economics Discussion Series*, No. 2024-067, Board of Governors of the Federal Reserve System. [101]

Kauko, K. et al. (2021), "Increased flood risks caused by climate change will also affect banks", *Bulletin Articles on the Economy*, Bank of Finland. [96]

Khairunisa, D. et al. (2023), "Public perception of flood risks in Klang Valley, Malaysia: A case study", *Sustainable Social Development*, Vol. 1/2, p. 2197, https://doi.org/10.54517/SSD.V1I2.2197. [22]

Khan, M., F. Johar and N. Baba (2017), "Disaster management risk perception of local communities", *Jurnal Kemanusiaan*, Vol. 26/1. [156]

Lema, R. (2025), *2025 Development in New York Insurance Law*, Phillips Lytle LLP. [128]

McKinsey & Company (Insurance Practice) (2024), *Global Insurance Report 2025: The pursuit of growth*, McKinsey & Company. [104]

McKinsey & Company (Insurance Practice) (2021), *2020 Global Insurance Pools statistics and trends: Distribution*, McKinsey & Company. [105]

Merry, A. and J. Rozo Calderon (2025), *The Landscape of Microinsurance: 2024*, Microinsurance Network. [114]

Merry, A. and J. Rozo Calderon (2023), *The Landscape of Microinsurance: 2022*, Microinsurance Network. [118]

Moody's (2025), *Climate-conditioned catastrophe models*, Moody's. [172]

Moody's (2025), *Cyclone, Hurricane & Typhoon Models*, Moody's. [37]

Moody's (2025), *Earthquake Models*, Moody's. [36]

Moody's (2025), *Global Flood Risk Models*, Moody's. [38]

Moody's (2025), *Severe Convective Storm Models*, Moody's. [39]

Mulya, A. (2023), *Basic Salary and Average Salary in Indonesia: 2023 Data*, Invest in Asia. [33]

NAIC (n.d.), *Catastrophe Modeling Center of Excellence*, National Association of Insurance Supervisors. [145]

Newman, R., J. Adams-Kane and K. Nicholls (2023), "2022 Flood Risk Assessment for Residential Mortgages", *RBNZ Bulletin*, No. 86-2, Reserve Bank of New Zealand. [97]

Norton Rose Fulbright (2024), *Insurance regulation in Asia Pacific 2024*, Norton Rose Fulbright. [134]

OECD (2025), *Insurance business written by class of insurance*, OECD Data Explorer, http://data-explorer.oecd.org/s/2ac. [48]

OECD (2024), *Consumer Finance Risk Monitor*, OECD Publishing, Paris, https://doi.org/10.1787/047b2ea6-en. [81]

OECD (2023), "Enhancing the insurance sector's contribution to climate adaptation", *Business and Finance Policy Papers*, Vol. 26. [143]

OECD (2023), "Leveraging technology in insurance to enhance risk assessment and policyholder risk reduction", *OECD Business and Finance Policy Papers*, No. 38, OECD, Paris, https://doi.org/10.1787/2f5c18ac-en. [125]

OECD (2021), *Enhancing Financial Protection Against Catastrophe Risks: The Role of Catastrophe Risk Insurance Programmes*, OECD Publishing, Paris, https://www.oecd.org/finance/insurance/Enhancing-financial-protection-against-catastrophe-risks.htm (accessed on 27 July 2022). [150]

OECD (2020), *Leveraging the Role of Property Catastrophe Reinsurance Markets: The Case of India, Indonesia, Myanmar, and the Philippines*, OECD, https://www.oecd.org/finance/insurance/leveraging-the-role-of-property-catastrophe-reinsurance-markets.htm (accessed on 15 July 2021). [148]

OECD (2020), *Recommendation of the Council on Financial Literacy*, OECD, https://legalinstruments.oecd.org/en/instruments/OECD-LEGAL-0461. [67]

OECD (2020), *Regulatory and Supervisory Framework for Insurance Intermediation*, OECD, https://www.oecd.org/content/dam/oecd/en/publications/reports/2020/03/regulatory-and-supervisory-framework-for-insurance-intermediation_e78a9ec5/19915a09-en.pdf. [109]

OECD (2018), *The Contribution of Reinsurance Markets to Managing Catastrophe Risk*, OECD, http://www.oecd.org/finance/the-contribution-of-reinsurance-markets-to-managing-catastrophe-risk.pdf (accessed on 23 January 2019). [45]

OECD (2013), "Policyholder Protection Schemes: Selected Considerations", *OECD Working Papers on Finance, Insurance and Private Pensions*, No. 31, OECD Publishing, Paris, https://doi.org/10.1787/5k46l8sz94g0-en. [84]

OJK (2024), *Insurance Statistics 2023*, Otoritas Jasa Keuangan. [129]

OJK (2021), *National Strategy on Indonesian Financial Literacy: 2021-2025*, Otoritas Jasa Keuangan. [25]

Paddam, S. et al. (2024), *Home Insurance Affordability and Home Loans at Risk*, Actuaries Institute. [158]

Pakistan Bureau of Statistics (2020), *Household Integrated Economic Surveys 2018-2019*, Pakistan Bureau of Statistics. [31]

Petrolia, D., C. Landry and K. Coble (2013), "Risk Preferences, Risk Perceptions, and Flood Insurance", *Land Economics*, Vol. 89/2, pp. 227-245, https://doi.org/10.3368/LE.89.2.227. [154]

Philippines Statistics Authority (2023), *Family Income and Expenditure Survey*, Philippines Statistics Authority. [32]

PIAM (2025), *About us*, Persatan Insurans Am Malaysia. [76]

PIDM (2025), *Coverage For TIPS*, Perbadanan Insurans Deposit Malaysia. [85]

PIRA (2021), *About us*, Philippine Insurers and Reinsurers Association. [78]

PIRA, I. (n.d.), *PIRA TV*, Philippine Insurers and Reinsurers Association. [80]

Poeschl, J. (2022), "Do banks manage their flood risk exposures? Evidence from the Danish credit register", *Economic Memo*, No. 15, Danmarks Nationalbank. [95]

Pratiwi, J. and F. Novaryani (2022), *Indonesia's Policy Guarantee to Restore Consumer Confidence in Insurers*. [90]

Property Rights Alliance (2024), *2024 International Property Rights Index: Countries*, Property Rights Alliance. [93]

Raman, M., A. Ojo and M. Dorasamy (2015), "A Stakeholder Perspective In Managing Floods In Malaysia", *WIT Transactions on The Built Environment*, Vol. 168, pp. 1171-1181, https://doi.org/10.2495/SD151012. [155]

Ren, J. and H. Wang (2016), "Rural Homeowners' Willingness to Buy Flood Insurance", *Emerging Markets Finance and Trade*, Vol. 52/5, pp. 1156-1166, https://doi.org/10.1080/1540496X.2015.1134867. [12]

Reynaud, A., M. Nguyen and C. Aubert (2018), "Is there a demand for flood insurance in Vietnam? Results from a choice experiment", *Environmental Economics and Policy Studies*, Vol. 20/3, pp. 593-617, https://doi.org/10.1007/S10018-017-0207-4/TABLES/7. [6]

Risk Frontiers (n.d.), *Natural Catastrophe Modelling*, Risk Frontiers. [42]

Royal, A. and M. Walls (2019), "Flood Risk Perceptions and Insurance Choice: Do Decisions in the Floodplain Reflect Overoptimism?", *Risk Analysis*, Vol. 39/5, pp. 1088-1104, https://doi.org/10.1111/RISA.13240. [7]

Sands, L. (2022), "Pakistan floods: One third of country is under water - minister", *BBC*, https://www.bbc.com/news/world-europe-62712301. [176]

SDIC (2018), *Scope of PPF Scheme Coverage*, Singapore Deposit Insurance Corporation. [86]

SECP (2024), *Insured Pakistan through Digitalization: Gaps, Potential & Roadmap*, Securities and Exchange Commission of Pakistan. [108]

SECP (2024), *Insured Pakistan: Pool Dynamics*, Securities and Exchange Commission of Pakistan. [136]

SECP (2024), *Journey to an Insured Pakistan: Five-Year Strategic Plan*, Securities and Exchange Commission of Pakistan. [103]

SECP (2024), *Reinsurance Performance Review 2023*, Securities and Exchange Commission of Pakistan. [168]

SECP (2024), *Report on Insurance Industry Statistics, 2023*, Securities and Exchange Commission of Pakistan. [55]

SECP (2024), *Unlocking the Potential of Micro and Inclusive Insurance in Pakistan*, Securities and Exchange Commission of Pakistan. [116]

SECP (2022), *Concept Paper: Proposed Risk Based Capital Regime for Pakistan's Insurance Sector*, Securities and Exchange Commission of Pakistan. [169]

SECP (2022), *Insurance Industry Statistics, 2021*, Securities and Exchange Commission of Pakistan. [54]

Seifert, I. et al. (2013), "Influence of flood risk characteristics on flood insurance demand: a comparison between Germany and the Netherlands", *Natural Hazards and Earth System Sciences*, Vol. 13/7, pp. 1691-1705, https://doi.org/10.5194/NHESS-13-1691-2013. [8]

Shah, S., I. Rana and A. Ali (2023), "Multi-hazard risk perception: An empirical study of the remote Gilgit city, Hindukush-Karakorum-Himalayan (HKH) region, Pakistan", *International Journal of Disaster Risk Reduction*, Vol. 96, p. 103996, https://doi.org/10.1016/J.IJDRR.2023.103996. [18]

Shaw, R. et al. (2023), "Asia", in *Climate Change 2022 – Impacts, Adaptation and Vulnerability*, Cambridge University Press, https://doi.org/10.1017/9781009325844.012. [1]

Souiden, N. and Y. Jabeur (2015), "The impact of Islamic beliefs on consumers' attitudes and purchase intentions of life insurance", *International Journal of Bank Marketing*, Vol. 33/4. [29]

State Bank of Pakistan (2025), *National Financial Inclusion Strategy: 2024-28.* [68]

Swiss Re Institute (2024), *World insurance: strengthening global resilience with a new lease of life*, Swiss Re. [24]

Tennyson, S. (2011), "Consumers' Insurance Literacy", No. 2011-PB-06, Networks Financial Institute. [173]

Uddin, M. (2017), "Microinsurance in India: Insurance literacy and demand", *Business and Economic Horizons*, Vol. 13/2, pp. 182-191, https://doi.org/10.15208/beh.2017.14. [66]

Valera, M., Z. Lei and J. Fong (2024), "Determinants of financial inclusion in Southeast Asia", *Applied Economics*, https://doi.org/10.1080/00036846.2024.2326529. [166]

Verisk Analytics (2025), *Verisk Peril Models.* [40]

Vinck, P. et al. (2024), *Information Sheet 3: Climate Change – Survey on Disaster Preparedness and Climate Change Perceptions in the Philippines.* [19]

Viverita, V. et al. (2014), "Households Perceptions on Factors Affecting Resilience towards Natural Disasters in Indonesia", *The South East Asian Journal of Management*, Vol. 8/1, p. 2, https://doi.org/10.21002/seam.v8i1.3099. [15]

Wachinger, G. et al. (2013), "The Risk Perception Paradox—Implications for Governance and Communication of Natural Hazards", *Risk Analysis*, Vol. 33/6, pp. 1049-1065, https://doi.org/10.1111/j.1539-6924.2012.01942.x. [10]

Wang, M. et al. (2012), "Are People Willing to Buy Natural Disaster Insurance in China? Risk Awareness, Insurance Acceptance, and Willingness to Pay", *Risk Analysis*, Vol. 32/10, pp. 1717-1740, https://doi.org/10.1111/J.1539-6924.2012.01797.X. [13]

Weedige, S. et al. (2019), "Decision Making in Personal Insurance: Impact of Insurance Literacy", *Sustainability*, Vol. 11/23, p. 6795, https://doi.org/10.3390/su11236795. [65]

Weerasuriya, W. and U. Rajapaksha (2023), "Effect of risk perception and vulnerability on adaptive architecture in flood resilience: a case from Ratnapura, Sri Lanka", *FARU Journal*, Vol. 10/1, pp. 49-58, https://doi.org/10.4038/faruj.v10i1.183. [17]

World Bank (2025), *World Bank Country and Lending Groups*, World Bank. [47]

World Bank (2023), *The Global Findex Database 2021*, World Bank. [106]

World Bank (n.d.), *Population, total.* [21]

World Bank and Bank Negara Malaysia (2024), *Managing Flood Risks: Leveraging Finance for Business Resilience in Malaysia*, World Bank. [34]

World Population Review (2025), *Home Ownership by Country 2025*, World Population Review. [164]

Yang, F., J. Tan and L. Peng (2020), "The effect of risk perception on the willingness to purchase hazard insurance—A case study in the Three Gorges Reservoir region, China", *International Journal of Disaster Risk Reduction*, Vol. 45, p. 101379, https://doi.org/10.1016/J.IJDRR.2019.101379. [5]

Notes

[1] It focuses, in particular, on the drivers of protection gaps and solutions in Indonesia, Malaysia, Pakistan, the Philippines and Sri Lanka. It has been developed with the collaboration of insurance regulators and supervisors in these five jurisdictions and benefitted from consultations with the insurance industry.

[2] For example, emerging and developing Asia and Pacific includes 6 of the 10 countries and 8 of the 20 countries deemed to face the highest natural hazard risk (the Philippines, Indonesia, India, Myanmar, Bangladesh, Pakistan, Papua New Guinea and Viet Nam) (Bündnis Entwicklung Hilft and IFHV, 2024[170]) and 3 of the 10 countries and 8 of the 20 counties most vulnerable to significant impacts from climate change (the Solomon Islands, Micronesia, Tonga, the Marshall Islands, Afghanistan, Tuvalu, Kiribati and the Maldives) (Chen et al., 2025[171]).

[3] A number of countries in the region, including Indonesia and the Philippines, have developed strategies to leverage the financial capacity of insurance and capital markets and reduce the financial burden on public finances.

[4] For the purposes of this study, "emerging and developing Asia and Pacific" includes all countries in Asia and Pacific classified as low income, lower middle income or upper middle income under the World Bank's Country and Lending Groups classification for 2025 (World Bank, 2025[47]).

[5] The collection and reporting of data on economic losses from natural hazards is likely to be less comprehensive in low-income countries, which could lead to an under-reporting of economic losses in those countries.

[6] In this ranking, exposure refers to "the nature and degree to which a system is exposed to significant climate change ....independent of socio economic context" (Chen et al., 2025[2]).

[7] This approach to measuring protection gaps likely overestimates the size of the gap as some types of losses are unlikely to be insured or intentionally uninsured (depending on the country). For example, in many countries, buildings and infrastructure owned by national or subnational governments are not insured by private insurance markets.

[8] The range reflects two approaches to measuring the share of losses insured: (i) including all available data on insured and economic losses; and (ii) including only loss years where both insured and economic loss estimates are provided.

[9] For countries classified as Low Income, almost all reported loss years did not include a reported insured loss.

[10] Based on (Cisternas et al., 2024[9]), risk awareness refers to the information or knowledge that households or businesses have about natural hazard risks and the potential for natural hazards to affect their community, whereas risk perception can be seen as referring to the outcome of the subjective evaluation by households and businesses of the likelihood that they could be impacted by a natural hazard. Risk perception is generally considered to be the primary basis for implementing preparedness measures (Cisternas et al., 2024[9]).

[11] Some regions of Malaysia are subject to frequent monsoon-related flooding with one estimate suggesting that 4.82 million Malaysians are affected by flooding annually (Raman, Ojo and Dorasamy, 2015[155]). A survey of individuals in the highly-populated Klang Valley found that 61% of respondents had experience with a flooding, including 28% that had experience with a flood in recent years and 7% that had experienced flooding more than three times (Khairunisa et al., 2023[22]).

[12] A significant portion of the country (75%) is located within the Indus river basin which has faced at least 14 major floods since 1947 (Abbas et al., 2015[157]) including the 2022 floods that reportedly submerged one third of the country (Sands, 2022[176]).

[13] The surveys were undertaken in eight European countries. A survey in France, Greece, Italy and Sweden found that an expectation of government compensation for losses was the main reason for not acquiring insurance for 4.8%, 4.9%, 9.6% and 14.7% of uninsured households (the share attributed to each country was not disclosed). Another survey in Belgium, Romania, Spain and Germany found that an expectation of government compensation for losses was the main reason for not acquiring insurance among 6% of respondents overall (EIOPA, 2024[4]).

[14] For the purposes of this limited review, a measure of "affordability stress" developed by the Actuaries Institute in Australia has been applied. The Actuaries Institute identifies households that face property

insurance premium costs above four weeks of gross household income as affordability-stressed (Paddam et al., 2024[158]). However, discretionary income (i.e. income remaining after accounting for cost-of-living expenses) is likely to be much higher in Australia and therefore the threshold for defining "affordability stress" should likely be lower than four weeks of gross household income in lower income countries.

15 Online offers of coverage are not found for household property insurance in Sri Lanka.

16 An assessment of natural hazard risk management practices is beyond the scope of this report.

17 For example, one of the major commercial providers of catastrophe models advertises the availability of climate-conditioned catastrophe models for a number of perils and regions, including for cyclones in the North Atlantic and Japan, flooding in Europe, Japan and the United States, windstorms in Europe and wildfires in the United States (Moody's, 2025[172]).

18 Catastrophe bonds are structured debt instruments that are used to fund reinsurance protection provided through a special-purpose entity that issues the bonds to investors (OECD, 2018[45]).

19 Collateralised reinsurance and sidecars are special-purpose reinsurance coverage providers that are fully funded by investors. Industry loss warranties are a type of reinsurance or derivative (option) contract that pays out when aggregate insurance industry losses from a catastrophic event exceed a pre-determined threshold (OECD, 2018[45]).

20 In proportional reinsurance, the premiums (and any claims) are shared proportionally and are therefore based on the pricing applied by the primary insurer. As a result, reinsurers that provide coverage on a proportional basis will seek to ensure that the pricing is adequate in order to avoid facing losses greater than premiums collected. If pricing is deemed to be inadequate, reinsurers are likely to decline coverage or propose coverage on a non-proportional basis.

21 For example, the Pakistan Reinsurance Corporation retroceded over 70% of the risk that they assumed in 2023 (SECP, 2024[168]).

22 Average based on data from (Helgi Library, 2025[159]) for available countries (99), classified based on World Bank's classification of countries by income (World Bank, 2025[47]). The dataset did not include estimates for Malaysia or Sri Lanka in 2021, so estimates for 2017 were used to calculate the average. Across high-income countries, approximately 23% of households own their home and have a mortgage (Everett-Allen, 2022[160]).

23 Based on (Helgi Library, 2025[159]). The dataset did not include estimates for Malaysia and Sri Lanka in 2021, so estimates for 2017 were used.

24 OECD calculations based on Helgi Library (2025[159]; 2025[161]; 2025[162]; 2025[163]).

25 OECD calculations based on (World Population Review, 2025[164]).

26 For example, in Malaysia and the Philippines, in particular, insurers reported substantial efforts to enhance the take-up of insurance coverage for natural hazard risks, partly driven by a need for increasing revenues to meet increased capital requirements in the case of the Philippines.

[27] In the case of business policyholders, the difference was substantially lower although remained significant.

[28] For example, requirements to offer earthquake coverage as part of residential property insurance coverage in California (United States) after the Northridge earthquake in 1994 led some insurers to withdraw from the property insurance market altogether.

[29] Some policyholders are required to purchase insurance in many countries (including Malaysia and the Philippines), such as households that reside in multi-tenant buildings given the impact that uninsured losses could have on other residents. In the Philippines, commercial establishments in high-risk zones are also required to acquire insurance against natural hazards in order to receive a business permit.

[30] Although some countries (e.g. Switzerland) have a legislative requirement to include coverage for natural hazards (or some natural hazards) in property insurance.

[31] An OECD review of regulatory and supervisory frameworks for insurance intermediaries found that only a few countries have restrictions on the distribution of some products through specific distribution channels, such as restrictions on the distribution of personal products by independent agents in Chile, Colombia, Israel, Latvia and Portugal and by banks in Colombia, Israel, Latvia and Portugal (OECD, 2020[109]).

[32] Financial exclusion is driven by a number of factors, including income and education as well as access to local financial services providers (among other factors) (Ayyagari and Beck, 2015[165]; Valera, Lei and Fong, 2024[166]; Hoque, Hossain and Siddique, 2023[167]).

[33] The Microinsurance Network's annual report on the microinsurance landscape reported a 4% increase in individuals covered by microinsurance between 2023 and 2024 (to 344 million) and a 6.8% increase in premiums collected (Merry and Rozo Calderon, 2025[114]).

[34] One recent microinsurance market analysis projected that the microinsurance market will grow by 6.5% annually between 2024 and 2032 (reported in (Insurance Asia, 2025[175])).

[35] One recent report estimated that the size of the global parametric insurance market was USD 16.2 billion in 2024 and is projected to grow at an annual rate of over 12% between 2025 and 2034 (Global Market Insights, 2025[124]).

[36] Wholly owned government agencies, such as the National Insurance Trust Fund, would not normally have an independent credit rating.

[37] In 2018, the OECD published an analysis of the role of international reinsurance markets in supporting post-disaster economic recovery. Using a unique set of data on property reinsurance premiums and claims provided by reinsurance companies, the OECD's report examined the impact of reinsurance on reducing the economic disruption in the aftermath of 26 major natural catastrophes (or series of natural catastrophes) that occurred between 2010 and 2016. The report found that, in countries where a relatively high share (10% or more) of economic losses related to the specific event(s) were reinsured, the post-event recovery occurred more quickly and these countries had higher than projected GDP growth in the following three years – while those countries with lower levels of reinsurance coverage struggled to recover and faced a cumulative loss in output relative to pre-event projections (OECD, 2018[45]).

[38] A number of countries also have risk sharing arrangements between governments and the insurance sector for agricultural risks. These programmes have not been included in the scope of this report.

[39] In Switzerland, there are two main approaches to providing property insurance that includes coverage for natural hazard risks. In some cantons, there are Public Insurance Companies for Real Estate that provide all property insurance to households and businesses and collaborate through a collective reinsurance arrangement. In other cantons, property insurance coverage is provided by private insurers who have established a co-insurance pool.

[40] In the United States, there is a National Flood Insurance Program that provides insurance for flood risks as well as a government-owned insurance company in the US state of California for earthquake risk. The Florida Hurricane Catastrophe Fund is a government agency that provides a reinsurance coverage to insurers in the US state of Florida. In addition, many US states have residual insurance programmes that provide property insurance for households (and sometimes businesses) that are unable to access insurance from private insurers. Some of the residual programmes (e.g. Florida, Louisiana) have been established as government-owned insurers.

[41] There are a number of public-private insurance programmes for agricultural risk (e.g. Philippines Crop Insurance Corporation, Crop Insurance Scheme in Sri Lanka) and for protecting public finances (e.g. Pooling Fund Bencana in Indonesia, parametric insurance for emergency funds and public asset insurance provided by the Government Service Insurance System in the Philippines) although these types of programmes have been excluded from the scope of this report.

[42] Maipark recently assumed an additional role in providing reinsurance coverage for government-owned assets.

[43] Insurance companies have been encouraged by the Insurance Commission to join the PCIF although membership is voluntary. At the time of writing, less than 50% of the non-life insurance companies in the Philippines have committed to join the PCIF (and some larger insurance companies have not joined the PCIF).

2 Protection gaps in retirement savings

This chapter analyses protection gaps in retirement savings in Asia by learning from the experiences of several countries. It looks at the extent to which protection gaps may arise from the rules of the pension system, the availability of savings and retirement income vehicles, and the population's use of the available vehicles. It then identifies the main drivers of the protection gaps and provides policy options to addressing those gaps.

Financial protection in old age is crucial for societies. There is usually a point in life when individuals' capacity to work and earn an income from work declines. Tools exist to provide financial protection in old age and ensure that individuals still get an income once retired so they can cover their living expenses. However, individuals are not always able or willing to use these tools. This can lead to financial protection gaps that can leave individuals under-protected and put their financial well-being at risk in retirement.

Several factors may lead to financial protection gaps in retirement savings. The first is the extent to which the regulatory framework establishes the appropriate savings and retirement income vehicles for individuals to adequately save for their retirement. This relates to the **rules** of the pension system that affect its capacity to deliver adequate retirement outcomes for the population. The second factor is the extent to which providers offer the savings and retirement income vehicles established in the regulatory framework for the population to use. This relates to the **availability** of appropriate savings instruments and vehicles. A final factor relates to the extent to which the population makes use of the available savings and retirement income vehicles to adequately prepare for their retirement. This relates to the population's uptake and **use** of the instruments at their disposal to save for retirement.

This chapter analyses financial protection gaps in retirement savings by looking at the experience of several Asian countries.[1] It first looks at financial protection gaps arising from the rules of the pension system, from the availability of savings and retirement income vehicles, and from the population's use of the available vehicles. It then discusses the main drivers of the financial protection gaps and provides policy options to addressing these gaps, using lessons learnt from those countries and OECD experiences. The analysis considers the direct measures of financial protection gaps, looking at the extent to which individuals have access to and contribute to savings and retirement income vehicles. It also considers broader challenges that may have an impact on the retirement income individuals receive, which is ultimately the measure of interest to assess financial protection gaps in retirement savings. Such additional challenges include issues related to investments, early access to savings or financial sustainability.

The analysis shows that financial protection gaps in retirement savings mainly originate from the fact that many individuals fail to participate in pension and retirement savings schemes, and when they do, the benefits they can expect to receive may be insufficient or may not cover them for their entire lifetime in retirement.

2.1. Protection gaps arising from the rules of the pension system

The capacity of the pension system to deliver adequate retirement outcomes depends on the rules of the system. The rules dictate to what extent individuals have access to pension and retirement savings schemes, how much they can contribute, how they can invest their savings, how they can access their savings, and how much they can expect as retirement income.

2.1.1. Coverage of pension and retirement savings schemes

Employees in the formal sector are usually covered by a mandatory pension scheme. Table 2.1 presents the types of pension schemes that different categories of workers have access to. In the seven countries analysed in this report (Indonesia, Malaysia, Pakistan, the Philippines, Sri Lanka, Thailand, Viet Nam), public-sector employees are mandatorily covered by a DB scheme, either tax financed or pay-as-you-go (PAYG). Malaysia and Sri Lanka distinguish between pensionable and non-pensionable public-sector employees, with a defined benefit (DB) scheme for the former and an asset-backed defined contribution (DC) scheme for the latter. Formal private-sector employees are usually covered by a mandatory contributory pension scheme, either PAYG DB or asset-backed DC. Indonesia, Pakistan, the Philippines and Sri Lanka also have mandatory DB severance systems for formal private-sector employees. Viet Nam is the only country with an integrated mandatory system for public and private-sector workers.

Table 2.1. Pension schemes' coverage by type of worker

Country	Name of pension scheme	Type of pension scheme	Public-sector employees	Private-sector employees	Self-employed & informal workers
Indonesia	Taspen – JP	PAYG DB (1)	M		
	Taspen – THT	Asset-backed DC	M		
	BPJS – JP	PAYG DB		M (2a)	
	BPJS – JHT	Asset-backed DC		M or V (2b)	V
	Retirement severance (PP)	Severance DB		M (3)	
	Employer pension funds (DPPK)	Asset-backed DB/DC		V	
	Financial institution pension funds (DPLK)	Asset-backed DC	V	V	V
Malaysia	Public service pension system (JPA)	PAYG DB (1)	M (5a)		
	Employee Provident Fund (EPF)	Asset-backed DC	M (5b)	M	V
	Private Retirement Schemes (PRS)	Asset-backed DC	V	V	V
Pakistan	Civil Service Pension Scheme (CSPS)	Tax-financed DB	M (6)		
	Employer Pension Funds (EPF)	Asset-backed DC	M (6)	V	
	Employees' Old-age Benefit Institute (EOBI)	PAYG DB		M (7)	
	Provident funds	Asset-backed DC		M (8)	
	Gratuity funds	Severance DB	M (6)	M (8)	
	Voluntary Pension System (VPS)	Asset-backed DC	V	V	V
Philippines	Government Service Insurance System (GSIS)	PAYG DB	M		
	Social Security System (SSS)	PAYG DB + Asset-backed DC (9)		M	M
	Retirement pay	Severance DB		M (10)	
	Occupational plans	Asset-backed DB/DC		V	
	Personal Equity and Retirement Accounts (PERA)	Asset-backed DC	V	V	V
Sri Lanka	Public Servants' Pension Scheme (PSPS)	Tax-financed DB	M (5a)		
	Public Servants' Provident Fund (PSPF)	Asset-backed DC	M (5b)		
	Employees' Provident Fund (EPF)	Asset-backed DC		M	
	Employees' Trust Fund (ETF)	Asset-backed DC	M (11)	M	
	Gratuity	Severance DB			
	Social Security Board (SSB)	Asset-backed DB			V
	Occupational plans	Asset-backed DC		V	
	Personal plans	Asset-backed DC	V	V	V
Thailand	Civil Service Pension (CSP)	Tax-financed DB	M		
	Government Pension Fund (GPF)	Asset-backed DC	M or V (12)		
	Social Security Fund (SSF) Article 33	PAYG DB		M	
	SSF Article 39	PAYG DB			V (13)
	SSF Article 40	Asset-backed DC			V
	National Savings Fund (NSF)	Asset-backed DC			V

Country	Name of pension scheme	Type of pension scheme	Public-sector employees	Private-sector employees	Self-employed & informal workers
	Provident Funds (PVD)	Asset-backed DC		V	
	Retirement Mutual Funds (RMF)	Asset-backed DC	V	V	V
Viet Nam	Viet Nam Social Security (VSS)	PAYG DB	M	M	M or V (14)
	Voluntary supplementary pensions	Asset-backed DC	V	V	V

Notes: M = mandatory; V = voluntary.
1. Employees contribute but benefits are financed by the government budget.
2a. Mandatory for employees of medium-sized and large enterprises. 2b. Mandatory for employees of small-sized, medium and large enterprises, and voluntary for employees of micro enterprises.
3. Only for permanent workers.
4. Including employees in micro-sized enterprises.
5a. Only for pensionable public-sector employees. 5b. For non-pensionable public-sector employees.
6. Some provinces are transitioning from tax-financed DB to asset-backed DC for civil servants.
7. Only for employees in companies with at least 10 employees. Employees working in financial institutions are not covered.
8. Only for employees in companies with at least 10 or 20 employees depending on the province. Employers can choose to set up a provident fund or a gratuity fund.
9. The asset-backed DC component only covers workers earning more than PHP 20 000 per month. Members also have access to a voluntary DC pension fund within the SSS.
10. Not mandatory for companies in the retail, services and agriculture sectors, as well as for employers with up to 10 employees.
11. Only for public-sector employees not in the government schemes (PSPS or PSPF).
12. Mandatory for those who joined the public service from 1997 and voluntary for the others.
13. Only for workers who have previously contributed to the mandatory scheme for private-sector employees.
14. Mandatory for business managers and owners of registered household businesses as of July 2025, and voluntary for farmers and informal sector workers.

In some countries, company size and type of sector influence the extent to which mandatory pension schemes cover formal private-sector employees. Among formal employees in Indonesia, 83% are working in large or medium enterprises,[2] 4% in small enterprises and 14% in micro enterprises. Only those working in large or medium-sized enterprises have access to the mandatory asset-backed DB scheme (BPJS – JP). In Pakistan, only private-sector workers in companies with at least 10 employees participate in the mandatory PAYG DB scheme (EOBI). This excludes 45% of persons employed in the informal sector and 38% of persons employed in the agricultural sector.[3] In the Philippines, private-sector employers with up to 10 employees and those in the retail, services and agriculture sectors are exempted from the obligation to provide a retirement severance scheme to their employees. More than 80% of employees in the Philippines work in those exempted sectors.[4] In Sri Lanka, only employees in companies with at least 15 employees may be eligible to gratuity.

Self-employed and informal workers represent a significant share of total workers, and they usually only have access to voluntary pension schemes. The share of self-employed and informal workers in total employment varies from 25% in Malaysia, to 33% in the Philippines, 41% in Sri Lanka, 44% in Viet Nam, 45% in Pakistan, 50% in Thailand and 59% in Indonesia.[5] The Philippines is the only country where these workers are mandatorily covered by the same pension scheme as private-sector employees (SSS). In Viet Nam, business managers and owners of registered household businesses are also covered by the same pension scheme as employees (VSS) as of July 2025. In the other countries, self-employed and informal workers only have access to voluntary pension schemes. In Indonesia and Malaysia, the self-employed can contribute on a voluntary basis to the mandatory asset-backed DC scheme covering private-sector employees (the BPJS – JHT and the EPF, respectively), though in Indonesia they are limited to the employee-portion of the mandatory contributions for formal workers. Sri Lanka has a voluntary asset-backed DB scheme (SSB) targeting the self-employed. In Thailand, workers who have contributed to the mandatory PAYG DB scheme (SSF Article 33) as formal private-sector employees are eligible to participate in a similar scheme (SSF Article 39) once they become self-employed or informal. Two other pension schemes target informal workers (SSF Article 40 and NSF).

All countries have voluntary personal pension plans, but occupational pension plans are not available everywhere. Voluntary personal pension plans are usually available to all workers.[6] By contrast, voluntary occupational pension plans are only accessible to the employees of the employers sponsoring the plans. Voluntary occupational pension plans are available in all countries except Malaysia. In Indonesia and the Philippines, these plans may be DB or DC and can be used to fully or partially offset employers' obligations under the DB severance scheme.[7] [8]

Additionally, citizens working abroad sometimes have access to pension schemes. In the Philippines, these workers are mandatorily covered by the same pension scheme as private-sector workers (SSS). Pakistan and Sri Lanka have dedicated voluntary pension schemes for workers abroad (within the VPS and SSB, respectively). Some countries also have special pension schemes for the armed forces and military personnel, such as Indonesia, Malaysia and the Philippines. These special arrangements are not covered further in this chapter.

Finally, safety net pensions are available for older people without access to other sources of income. Table 2.2 shows that, depending on the country, the programmes may target people over the age of 60 (Malaysia, the Philippines, Thailand) or those over the age of 70 (Indonesia, Sri Lanka and Viet Nam). All the programmes are means-tested to target only the elderly with no or low resources.

Table 2.2. Safety net programmes for the elderly

	Programme description
Indonesia	The Elderly Social Rehabilitation Assistance Programme (ATENSI LU) is a tax-financed programme providing social assistance for the elderly, including financial assistance to meet basic needs. The Family Hope Programme for the Elderly (PKH Lansia) is a means-tested, quarterly social pension for people aged 70+.
Malaysia	The Old-Age Assistance programme (BWE) provides a means-tested monthly benefit of MYR 600 to individuals aged 60+ in households falling below the poverty line.
Philippines	The Social Pension for Indigent Senior Citizens (SPISC) provides a monthly benefit of PHP 1 000 to people aged 60+ who are sick or disabled, without a permanent source of income and without regular support from family or relatives.
Pakistan	No specific programme for the elderly but the Benazir Income Support Programme (BISP) is a social protection programme for low-income groups.
Sri Lanka	The Senior Citizen Allowance for Strengthen Elderly provides people aged 70+ with a monthly income below LKR 3 000 with a monthly allowance of LKR 2 000.
Thailand	The Old Age Allowance is a means-tested programme for people aged 60+ not receiving a civil service pension.
Viet Nam	Vietnamese citizens aged 75 and above who do not receive a pension or monthly social insurance benefits and make a written request are entitled to the social pension. In addition, Vietnamese citizens aged 70 to 74 who are classified as poor or near-poor and meet the above conditions (not receiving monthly pension or social insurance benefits and making a written request) are also entitled to the social pension. The monthly social pension is VND 500 000 as of 1 July 2025.

Significant portions of the population are out of the labour force, in particular among women, making them reliant on safety net programmes. Figure 2.1 shows that the labour force participation rate of women varies from 21% to 63% across the Asian countries covered, while it stands at 67% in the OECD area. Moreover, labour force participation rates are much larger for men. This implies that women are less likely to be covered by the pension system and to build their own pension entitlements, leaving them with only safety net pensions. In some countries, individuals outside the labour force have access to voluntary pension schemes, however. For example, in Malaysia, any individual outside the labour force can voluntarily participate in the mandatory scheme for private-sector employees (EPF). In addition, male members of the EPF can divert two percentage points of their own mandatory contributions to their wife's account, as long as their wife is also an EPF member. In the Philippines, non-working spouses of members of the mandatory pension scheme for private-sector employees (SSS) can voluntarily participate in the scheme. In Sri Lanka, parents can enrol their children aged under 18 in a pension scheme (SSB).

Figure 2.1. Labour force participation rate, by gender

As a percentage of the population aged 15 and over

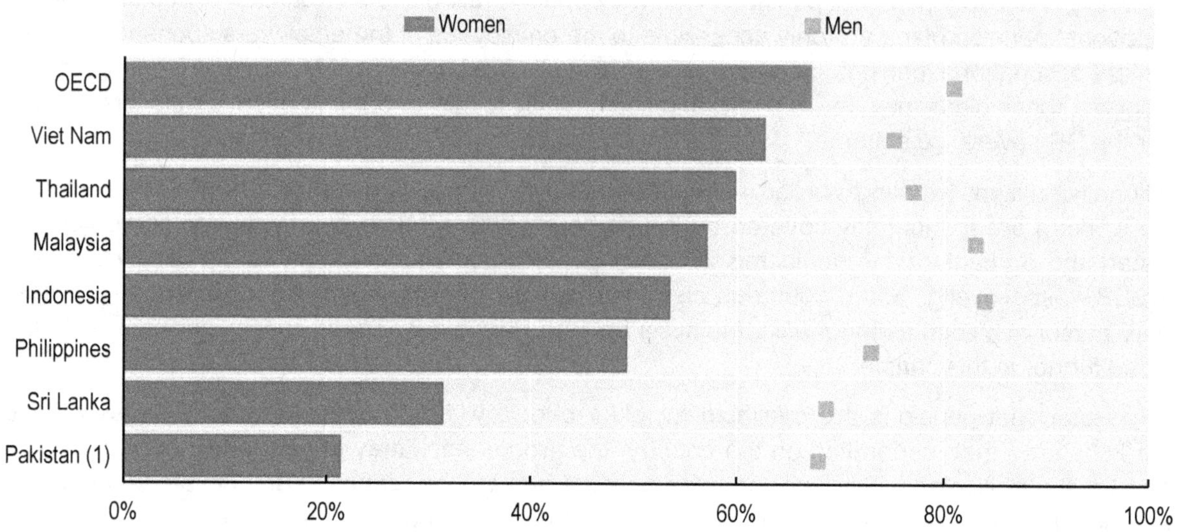

Note: 1. Ratio as a percentage of the population aged 10 and over.
Source: Labour Force Surveys and OECD Labour force participation rate database.

2.1.2. Contribution rules

Mandatory contribution rates vary across countries and categories of workers. Figure 2.2 shows that mandatory contribution rates are set at 20% of earnings or more for some categories of workers in Malaysia (24% for private-sector employees), Pakistan (22% for civil servants in the Khyber Pakhtunkhwa or KPK province), the Philippines (21% for private-sector employees), Sri Lanka (23% for private-sector employees) and Viet Nam (22% for public and private-sector employees). By contrast, mandatory contribution rates are below 10% in Indonesia and Thailand for both public and private-sector employees, as well as in Pakistan for private-sector employees. In Pakistan, the Philippines and Thailand, contribution rates are higher for public than for private-sector employees, while it is the other way around in Indonesia, Malaysia and Sri Lanka. Contributions are usually shared between employers and employees, except in Indonesia (only public-sector employees contribute to their mandatory pension schemes, Taspen) and Malaysia (only the government contributes to the mandatory pension scheme for public-sector employees, JPA). By way of comparison, mandatory contribution rates average 20% of earnings across OECD countries for private-sector employees, with 41% paid by employees on average. In the Philippines, the self-employed must contribute by themselves as much as in the case of private-sector employees (15% in the SSS), but they declare the income on which contributions are calculated and tend to set it at the minimum (PHP 5 000 per month in 2025).[9] In Viet Nam too, the self-employed mandatorily covered by the pension scheme for employees must pay the full contribution by themselves (22% in the VSS).

Figure 2.2. Mandatory contribution rates for public and private-sector employees, split between employer and employee shares

As a percentage of earnings

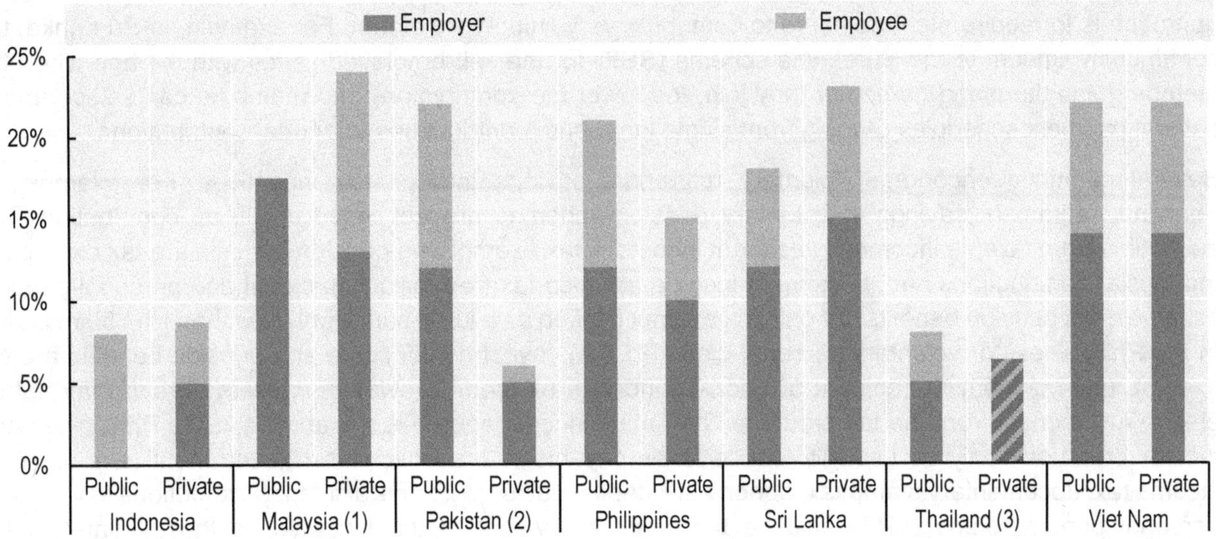

Notes:
1. The contribution rate of 24% shown for private-sector employees (11% paid by employees and 13% paid by employers) applies to Malaysians and permanent resident workers under the age of 60 and earning up to MYR 5 000 per month. An employer contribution rate of 12% instead of 13% applies for those earning more than MYR 5 000 per month. For permanent resident workers aged 60 and above, all contribution rates are halved. For Malaysians aged 60 and above, a 4% contribution rate applies and is fully paid by the employer.
2. Data for public-sector employees refer to the Khyber Pakhtunkhwa (KPK) province.
3. For private-sector employees, the 6.35% contribution rate is jointly paid by the employer, the employee and the government.

Mandatory contributions may apply on a portion of earnings when earnings subjected to mandatory contributions are capped. In Indonesia, contributions to the mandatory asset-backed DB scheme for private-sector employees (BPJS – JP) are calculated on earnings up to IDR 10 547 000 per month (3.3 times the average wage). In Pakistan, contributions to the mandatory pension scheme for private-sector employees (EOBI) are calculated based on the minimum wage. In the Philippines, contributions to the mandatory pension scheme for private-sector workers (SSS) are calculated on earnings up to PHP 20 000 per month (1.1 time the average wage) for the PAYG DB component and on earnings between PHP 20 000 and PHP 35 000 per month (1.9 time the average wage) for the asset-backed DC component. At the end of 2023, around one-third of active SSS members had earnings above the first threshold and were contributing to the DC fund. In Viet Nam, the cap on earnings corresponds to 20 times the reference level or VND 46.8 million per month as of July 2024 (6.2 times the average wage).

Voluntary contributions may be associated with minimum and maximum limits. Such limits may be expressed as a percentage of income or as a fixed amount. For example, in Sri Lanka and Thailand, public-sector employees can top up their contributions to the mandatory asset-backed DC scheme by up to 6% of salary in Sri Lanka (PSPF) and between 1% and 27% of salary in Thailand (GPF). In Thailand, employee contributions to voluntary occupational DC schemes can be between 2% and 15% of salary and the same range applies to employer contributions. In countries expressing the maximum limit as a fixed amount, that amount ranges from a few percentage points of the national average wage (e.g. THB 300 per month or 2% of the average wage in Thailand for informal workers contributing to the SSF Article 40) to several multiples of the national average wage (e.g. PHP 400 000 per year or 181% of the average wage in the

Philippines for workers abroad contributing to a PERA). When contribution floors are set as a fixed amount, this amount represents no more than 0.2% of the national average wage.

While contributions to voluntary occupational pension schemes must be paid monthly, more flexibility is granted to contributions to voluntary personal pension schemes in some countries. For example, in the Philippines, individuals contributing to a PERA can choose how often to pay contributions. Another approach is to require plan members to contribute very little every month. For example, in Sri Lanka, the contribution amount to the Surekuma scheme (SSB) for the self-employed varies with the age when the member joins the plan (the earlier they join, the lower the contribution) and members can select among several payment schedules ranging from single lump-sum contributions to annual contributions.

Several countries encourage voluntary retirement savings through tax incentives. For example, in Thailand, retirement savings in voluntary pension schemes are not taxed at all, as contributions are deductible from taxable income, investment income is tax exempt and pension benefits are tax exempt. In Indonesia, contributions and investment income are also tax free for occupational and personal pension schemes, but pension benefits are only tax exempt if taken as a lump sum worth less than IDR 50 million.[10] In the Philippines, for voluntary personal plans (PERA), investment income and pension benefits are tax exempt, and contributions enjoy a 5% non-refundable tax credit. However, workers abroad may not be able to fully benefit from the tax credit, as their main income source is not taxable in the Philippines and the tax credit can only be used to reduce taxes payable to the Philippines' government (e.g. personal income tax, documentary stamp tax, donor's tax, capital gains tax).[11] In Pakistan, contributions to voluntary personal pension plans (VPS) enjoy a tax credit equivalent to the tax paid on those contributions, investment income is tax exempt and 50% of the accumulated assets can be taken as a tax-free lump sum, with the rest being taxed at the average tax rate over the past three years.[12] The tax treatments described above tend to be more generous than the most common one applying in OECD countries, where contributions are tax deductible, investment income is tax exempt and pension benefits are taxable (OECD, 2024[1]).

Another approach used in some countries to encourage voluntary retirement savings is through state matching contributions. Tax deductions and non-refundable tax credits on contributions only provide an incentive to individuals paying personal income tax. However, many individuals may not pay personal income tax.[13] Alternatively, state matching contributions are valuable irrespective of the tax status of the individual. In Malaysia, members of the mandatory asset-backed DC scheme for private-sector employees (EPF) who are self-employed workers or female registered in the National Poverty Data Bank are eligible for state matching contributions (20% and 50%, respectively, subject to an annual and lifetime cap) if they make voluntary contributions. Thailand has two pension schemes targeting informal workers and encouraging voluntary contributions through state matching contributions. In the national savings fund (NSF), the match rate increases with age, from 50% for members aged 15 to 30, to 80% for those aged 31 to 50 and to 100% for those aged 51 to 60. For the SSF Article 40, benefits may include old-age support depending on the option selected by the members. For options that include old-age benefits, the state provides a matching contribution of either THB 50 or THB 150 per month (effectively a 50% match rate).[14] Ten OECD countries also use state matching contributions to encourage retirement savings (OECD, 2024[2]).

2.1.3. Investment rules

Investment rules may lead to significant concentration risk and low investment performance over the long term as they tend to favour secured assets for the investment of retirement savings and public pension reserves. For example, in Indonesia, voluntary pension funds (DPPK and DPLK) must invest a minimum of 30% in Indonesian government bonds. In Malaysia, the mandatory asset-backed DC scheme for private-sector employees (EPF) is required to invest or re-invest at least 50% of funds into domestic government bonds, subject to a minimum of 70% of total assets invested in such assets, according to the EPF Act

1991.[15] In the Philippines, the asset-backed DC scheme and the reserves of the PAYG DB scheme for private-sector workers (SSS) must have at least 15% of their assets in domestic government bonds, while listed equities cannot exceed 40% of the assets of the DB reserves and 20% of the assets of the DC scheme. In Sri Lanka, the mandatory asset-backed DC scheme for public and private-sector workers (ETF) should maintain an asset allocation of minimum 94% in fixed income securities and maximum 6% in equities. In Thailand, at least 60% of the assets of the reserve fund of the PAYG DB schemes for private-sector workers (SSF Article 33 and Article 39) must be invested in highly secured assets, i.e. cash and deposits, government bonds and corporate bonds guaranteed by the state or with investment grade, while foreign investment cannot exceed 47% of total assets. Similarly, the reserves for the tax-financed DB scheme for public-sector employees (CSP) can only be invested in cash and deposits, government bonds and debt instruments issued by the Thai Ministry of Finance or state enterprises. In Viet Nam, voluntary pension funds must invest at least 50% of their portfolios in domestic government bonds. By contrast, no OECD country imposes an investment floor in domestic government bonds for pension funds (OECD, 2024[3]).

Plan members have limited investment choice in mandatory asset-backed DC schemes. There is no investment choice in Indonesia (Taspen – THT and BPJS – JHT), Pakistan (provident funds and employer pension funds), the Philippines (SSS) and Sri Lanka (EPF, ETF and PSPF). This could be linked to the fact that guarantees apply in some of these countries. Indeed, there is a 2.5% annual return guarantee in Sri Lanka. In Indonesia, the minimum guaranteed return is equal to the average interest rate of the 1-year counter rate of government bank deposit. In the Philippines, there is a capital guarantee at the time of retirement. By contrast, plan members have investment choice in Malaysia and Thailand. In Malaysia, members of the EPF can choose between a conventional fund and a sharia fund. The conventional fund is the default option and benefits from a 2.5% annual return guarantee. Moreover, EPF members who have saved above a certain threshold can transfer 30% of their excess savings to the i-Invest platform and choose their own investments from an approved list. In Thailand, public-sector employees who are members of the GPF can choose among several investment options.

Within occupational DC pension plans, employers may not always offer investment choice to participating employees. For example, in Thailand, a fund committee composed of employee and employer representatives approves all the parameters of the occupational pension plan (PVD), including whether to provide investment choice to members and, if so, the default investment strategy. Given the general low risk tolerance of Thai people and low levels of financial knowledge among fund committee members, most fund committees select a conservative strategy for all members or for the default option. At the end of 2022, 57% of employers provided occupational plans with investment choice for members and 4% of them offered a life-cycle investment option (ThaiPVD, 2022[4]).

By contrast, investment choice is usually provided in voluntary personal pension schemes. There are some exceptions. For example, in the Philippines, the voluntary pension scheme for the members of the SSS does not provide investment choice. In Thailand, members of the voluntary personal pension plans for informal workers do not have investment choice (NSF and SSF Article 40).

Some countries regulate the type of investment options offered to members of DC pension schemes. Table 2.3 shows that this is the case in Indonesia, Malaysia, Pakistan and the Philippines. In Malaysia, Pakistan and Thailand, the default option is a life-cycle investment strategy, although in Pakistan pension fund managers are not obliged to offer this type of investment option and may therefore select another default. Life-cycle investment strategies are also the preferred default option in the OECD (OECD, 2020[5]).

Table 2.3. Investment options in DC pension schemes

	Type of scheme	Mandatory investment options	Default investment option
Indonesia	DPPK (DC) and DPLK	Four investment profiles for employee contributions, including a life-cycle strategy	No default option
Malaysia	PRS	Growth, moderate, and conservative funds + life-cycle strategy	Life-cycle strategy
Pakistan	VPS	High Volatility, Medium Volatility, Low Volatility, and Lower Volatility allocations (1)	- Life Cycle Allocation - Low Volatility or Lower Volatility allocations if Life Cycle Allocation not provided
Philippines	PERA	Only Unit Investment Trust Funds (UITF) are currently available in the market	No default option
Thailand	GPF		Life-cycle strategy

Note: 1. The allocations represent different combinations of investment in minimum three mandatory sub-funds (equity, debt and money market).

2.1.4. Early access to retirement savings

Members of asset-backed DC schemes can usually withdraw their savings before the normal age of retirement, although some conditions and penalties may apply. Table 2.4 presents the conditions to access DC retirement savings before the normal age of retirement. Malaysia and the Philippines are the only two countries where at least part of the mandatory retirement savings cannot be accessed before retirement age.[16] In Indonesia, Pakistan, Sri Lanka and Thailand, plan members changing or losing jobs may be able to withdraw their savings, even from mandatory schemes in the first three countries. In most countries, plan members reaching a certain age (below the normal age of retirement), a minimum length of membership or with a minimum number of years of contributions can also withdraw their savings. Access to retirement savings may also be granted when plan members fulfil certain conditions (e.g. total and permanent disability, leaving the country, getting married) or when they need money to cover specific expenses (e.g. health, housing, education). Retirement savings may also be available at any time from voluntary schemes, although tax penalties apply. For example, in the Philippines, withdrawing PERA contributions without complying with the minimum age (55 years old) and contribution duration (5 years) leads to the repayment to the tax authority of all the tax incentives provided to the individual, i.e. the tax credit on his/her contributions, the tax exemption of employer contributions, and the tax exemption of investment income.

Table 2.4. Conditions to access DC retirement savings before the normal age of retirement

	Pension scheme	Not possible	Leave job	Reach minimum age/membership	Special conditions	Outside previous conditions
Indonesia	BPJS – JHT		Need at least 5 years of contributions		Permanent total disability	
	Occupational and personal plans			50 years old	DPLK: Financial hardship, critical illness, giving up Indonesian nationality, foreign citizen leaving the country	
Malaysia	EPF	Retirement account (up to age 55)		Well-being account: 50 years old	All accounts: Incapacitation, leaving the country, civil servants achieving pensionable status Well-being account: Education, housing, health, Hajj	Flexible account and savings above MYR 1 million
	PRS				Emigration, housing, health	Tax penalties
Pakistan	Provident funds		Yes		Depends on the employer	
	VPS			25 years of membership		Tax penalties
Philippines	SSS	Mandatory account		Voluntary account: 1 year of membership	Voluntary account: Critical illness, involuntary separation from employment and repatriation of overseas Filipino workers	
	PERA			55 years old and 5 years of contributions	Hospitalisation, disability	Tax penalties
Sri Lanka	PSPF		End of contract		Health, marriage (women)	
	EPF		Starting employment in public service	10 years of contributions and min asset level: Housing, health	Marriage (women), disability, emigration	
	ETF		Cessation of employment	60 years old	Emigration, disability	
	SSB				At request if unable to continue to pay contributions	
Thailand	PVD and RMF		Tax penalties			Tax penalties
Viet Nam	Voluntary supplementary pensions				Disability, illness	

Note: Mandatory pension schemes are in blue and voluntary pension schemes are in orange.

Some countries allow plan members to take loans from their mandatory pension schemes. This is the case in the Philippines and Sri Lanka. In the Philippines, public and private-sector workers can take loans from their respective mandatory pension schemes (GSIS and SSS). For public-sector employees, the interest rate on the loan varies from 6% to 10% depending on the type of loan, while for private-sector workers, a fixed interest rate of 10% applies. In case of a default on a loan, deductions are made from the pension benefit payments received at retirement. In Sri Lanka, private-sector employees who are active members of the EPF can use 75% of their account as collateral for a housing loan. If members fail to pay the due instalments, the outstanding obligation (unpaid instalments plus a surcharge interest) is deducted from the account balance. Only few OECD countries allow plan members to take loans from their pension plan (e.g. Canada, Poland, the United States) (OECD, 2019[6]).

2.1.5. Expected pension benefits

The formulas to calculate pension benefits in mandatory DB pension schemes tend to be more generous to public-sector employees than to private-sector employees. Table 2.5 shows that, in Indonesia, Pakistan, the Philippines and Thailand, public and private-sector employees are covered by different DB pension schemes and the accrual rate is always higher for the former. Moreover, the formula uses the final salary for public-sector employees in Indonesia and Malaysia, and in Thailand for those hired prior to 1997. For private-sector employees, the formula usually uses an average salary over a period ranging from five years in Thailand and the Philippines, to the full career in Indonesia. In Viet Nam, women benefit from a higher accrual rate than men for the initial years of participation as they are entitled to a monthly pension equal to 45% of their average salary with 15 years of participation (3% yearly accrual rate), while men need to contribute for 20 years to reach the same benefit level (2.25% yearly accrual rate).[17]

Table 2.5. Benefit formula for mandatory DB pension schemes

	Sector	Yearly accrual rate	Salary	Minimum benefit	Maximum benefit	Minimum number of years of service
Indonesia	Public (Taspen – JP)	2.5%	Final basic salary	45% of final basic salary	80% of final basic salary	15 years
	Private (BPJS – JP)	1%	Weighted average annual salary over the contribution period, adjusted for inflation	IDR 300 000	IDR 3 600 000	15 years for a pension; lump sum otherwise
Malaysia	Public (JPA)	..	Final salary	MYR 1 000 with at least 25 years of service	60% of final salary after 30 years of service	10 years
Pakistan	Public (CSPS) (1)	2.33%	Average salary over past 1 to 3 years	PKR 10 000 to PKR 17 000	70% of average salary after 30 years of service	10 to 25 years for a pension
	Private (EOBI)	2%	Average minimum wage over past 12 months	PKR 10 000	PKR 30 000	2 years for a lump sum; 15 years for a pension
Philippines	Public (GSIS)	2.5%	Average salary over past 36 months		90% of average salary	3 years for a lump sum; 15 years for a pension
	Private (SSS)	2%	Average salary over past 60 months	Highest of 40% of average salary or PHP 1 200 (respectively PHP 2 400) with at least 10 credited years of service (respectively 20)	Salary capped at PHP 20 000 / month in formula	10 years for a pension; lump sum otherwise
Sri Lanka	Public (PSPS)	..	Final salary		85-90% of final salary after 30 years of service	10 years

	Sector	Yearly accrual rate	Salary	Minimum benefit	Maximum benefit	Minimum number of years of service
Thailand	Public (CSP)	2%	Hired before 1997: Final salary; Hired from 1997: Average salary over past 5 years			10 years for a lump sum; 25 years for a pension
	Private (SSF Article 33 and Article 39)	1.3% then 1.5% beyond 15 years of participation	Average salary over past 5 years		Salary capped at THB 15 000 / month in formula	15 years for a pension; lump sum otherwise
Viet Nam	Public and private (VSS)	Females: 3% then 2% beyond 15 years of participation Males: 2.25% then 2% beyond 20 years of participation or 2.7% then 1% beyond 15 years of participation but less than 20	Career average salary (2)		75% of average salary capped at 20 times the reference level	15 years for a pension; lump sum otherwise

Notes: ".." means not available. This table includes all mandatory DB pension schemes, irrespective of the financing method (PAYG, tax-financed or asset-backed).

1. The number of years considered for the average salary, the minimum number of years of service and the minimum benefit vary across provinces.

2. For public-sector employees who joined the public service before January 2025, the average salary is calculated on the past 5 to 20 years depending on when they joined, instead of the full career.

Ceilings on pension benefits may become increasingly restrictive. Some countries have a ceiling on the benefits that DB schemes pay, either through a maximum benefit level in nominal terms (e.g. BPJS in Indonesia, EOBI in Pakistan) or through a cap on the earnings used in the formula (e.g. SSS in the Philippines, SSF in Thailand, VSS in Viet Nam) (Table 2.5). This reduces expected replacement rates for higher-income earners. Moreover, these ceilings may not be indexed to wage growth. For example, the earnings cap of THB 15 000 per month in Thailand has been fixed at this level since 1999. In the Philippines, the PHP 20 000 earnings cap has not been adjusted at least since 2019. This means that the cap becomes restrictive for a growing proportion of members over time. Similarly, in Indonesia, while the maximum benefit level is indexed to prices, it could become restrictive if wages grow faster than prices. In Viet Nam, the reference level used to cap earnings is adjusted in line with inflation and economic growth, considering the state budget's capacity and the financial position of the social insurance fund.

Mandatory DB pension schemes usually require a vesting period, so workers usually need to contribute for a minimum number of years to get a pension benefit at retirement. The minimum service period requirement to get a pension varies from 10 to 25 years across countries and types of schemes (Table 2.5). In the Philippines and Thailand, public-sector employees must participate for longer in their scheme than private-sector employees to be entitled to pension benefits. In Pakistan, the Philippines (GSIS) and Thailand (CSP), there is a lower threshold to get entitled to a lump sum instead of a pension. In Indonesia (BPJS – JP), the Philippines (SSS), Thailand (SSF) and Viet Nam (VSS), individuals not fulfilling the minimum service period receive a lump sum.

The retirement age currently varies across countries between 50 and 61 years old, depending on the type of pension scheme. Generally, different retirement ages apply to different types of pension schemes, except in Malaysia where a single retirement age of 60 applies (Table 2.6). In Indonesia, retirement ages are higher for DB schemes than for DC schemes (currently 59 versus 56). The retirement age is lower for voluntary pension schemes than for mandatory ones in Indonesia and the Philippines. In general, the same retirement age applies to public and private-sector employees in their respective mandatory scheme, except in Thailand, where public-sector employees have a higher retirement age (60 versus 55). Pakistan, Sri Lanka and Viet Nam have a lower retirement age for females than for males at least in some of the pension schemes. In Indonesia, the retirement age in the mandatory DB schemes for public and private-sector employees is increasing gradually from 56 in 2015 to 65 by 2043. In Viet Nam, the retirement ages in the mandatory DB scheme for public and private-sector employees have been increasing since January 2021 by 3 months per year for men to reach 62 in 2028, and by 4 months per year for women to reach 60 in 2035.

Table 2.6. Normal retirement ages

	50	55	56	59	60	61
Indonesia		- VO - VP	- MDC public and private-sector employees	- MDB public and private-sector employees (1)		
Malaysia					All schemes (2)	
Pakistan		- MDB private-sector employees (female)			- MDB public and private-sector employees (male) - VO - VP	
Philippines	- VO	- VP			- MDB public and private-sector employees	
Sri Lanka	- MDC private-sector employees (female)	- MDB and MDC public-sector employees - MDC private-sector employees (male)			- MDC public and private-sector employees - VDB self-employed workers	
Thailand		- MDB private-sector employees - VDB informal workers - VO - VP			- MDB and MDC public-sector employees - VDC informal workers	
Viet Nam			Female (3) - MDB public and private-sector employees - VO - VP			Male (4) - MDB public and private-sector employees (male) - VO - VP

Notes: "VO" = voluntary occupational scheme; "VP" = voluntary personal scheme; "MDC" = mandatory DC scheme; "MDB" = mandatory DB scheme; "VDC" = voluntary DC scheme; "VDB" = voluntary DB scheme.
1. Increasing gradually every three years until reaching 65 by 2043.
2. The retirement age is 60 for pensionable civil servants appointed since 2012. They may opt for early retirement at the earliest at 55. For private-sector employees, the retirement age is also 60 but members of the mandatory pension scheme (EPF) can withdraw their savings from age 55. Contributions made after age 55 are locked in until age 60.
3. Increasing gradually to 60 by 2035.
4. Increasing gradually to 62 by 2028.

Members of mandatory DB schemes may be entitled to a lifelong pension at retirement, protecting them from the risk of longevity. In the seven countries, workers fulfilling the conditions regarding the contribution period and the retirement age are entitled to a lifelong pension from mandatory DB pension schemes. They also get a lump sum in addition to their lifelong pension in the Philippines (for public-sector employees), Sri Lanka (for public-sector employees) and Viet Nam (with more than 35 or 30 years of participation for men and women, respectively). In Pakistan (for public-sector employees) and the Philippines (for private-sector workers), workers can substitute part of their pension for a lump sum. Workers not fulfilling the minimum contribution period are usually entitled to a lump sum at retirement. However, they may not receive any benefit such as in the Philippines and Thailand, where public-sector employees should have at least 3 and 10 years of service, respectively, to get a lump sum (Table 2.5), or in Malaysia where benefits are forfeited if resigning before the age of 40 with less than 10 years of public service.

Members of mandatory asset-backed DC schemes are not protected against longevity risk. In most cases, workers are only entitled to a lump sum at retirement. Monthly instalments are also available in Malaysia (in the EPF) and the Philippines (over fixed periods of 5, 10 or 15 years in the SSS). Occupational and personal voluntary pension schemes tend to offer a range of options at retirement, including lump sums, drawdowns and annuities. In Indonesia, the payment of pension benefits from occupational pension plans must be made periodically over at least 10 years through drawdowns or annuities, and only 20% can be taken as a lump sum.[18] Similarly, in Viet Nam, monthly payments from voluntary supplementary pension plans must last at least 10 years.

Similarly, severance DB schemes only pay a lump sum at retirement. These schemes exist in Indonesia, Pakistan, the Philippines and Sri Lanka. Benefits are proportional to the number of years of service with the employer.[19] In the Philippines, employees need at least five years of service with the employer from whom they retire to receive a retirement severance payment. Similarly, in Indonesia, only the years of service with the employer from whom they retire count for the calculation of the benefits. In Pakistan, employees need at least six months of service to be entitled to severance benefits, which they receive whenever they leave their employer. In Sri Lanka, employees who have completed a minimum 5 years of continuous service with the same employer receive their gratuity payment within 30 days of the termination of their service.

Lack of portability between different pension schemes may impede the ability of workers switching jobs to accrue pension rights for their full career. For example, in Thailand, employees moving between public and private-sector employment accumulate pension rights under the civil service pension and the SSF Article 33 separately. Because of this separation, they may fail to fulfil the required minimum contribution period under each scheme to receive lifetime pension benefits. In Indonesia and the Philippines, the severance retirement pay is fully paid by the last employer and calculated based on the number of years of service with that employer only. In the Philippines and Sri Lanka, entitlement to severance benefits also requires a minimum of five years of service with the employer. This disadvantages mobile private-sector workers.

The length of time in retirement is longer for women than for men, which may lead to lower pension benefits from asset-backed DC schemes. Women's longer average life expectancy means that, for a given age of retirement, they will spend more time in retirement than men and their assets will need to finance a longer period (Figure 2.3). According to 2024 data, women are expected to spend between 2.5 and 5.2 more years in retirement than men. Additionally, differences in time spent in retirement are even greater when women can retire earlier than men. For example, in Sri Lanka, private-sector employees can get a lump sum from the mandatory asset-backed DC scheme (EPF) from age 50 for women and 55 for men. This implies that women have lower contribution periods leading to lower lump sums, which need to finance a longer retirement period of 33 years for women, as opposed to 24 years for men.

Figure 2.3. Length of the retirement period according to the normal age of retirement

In years

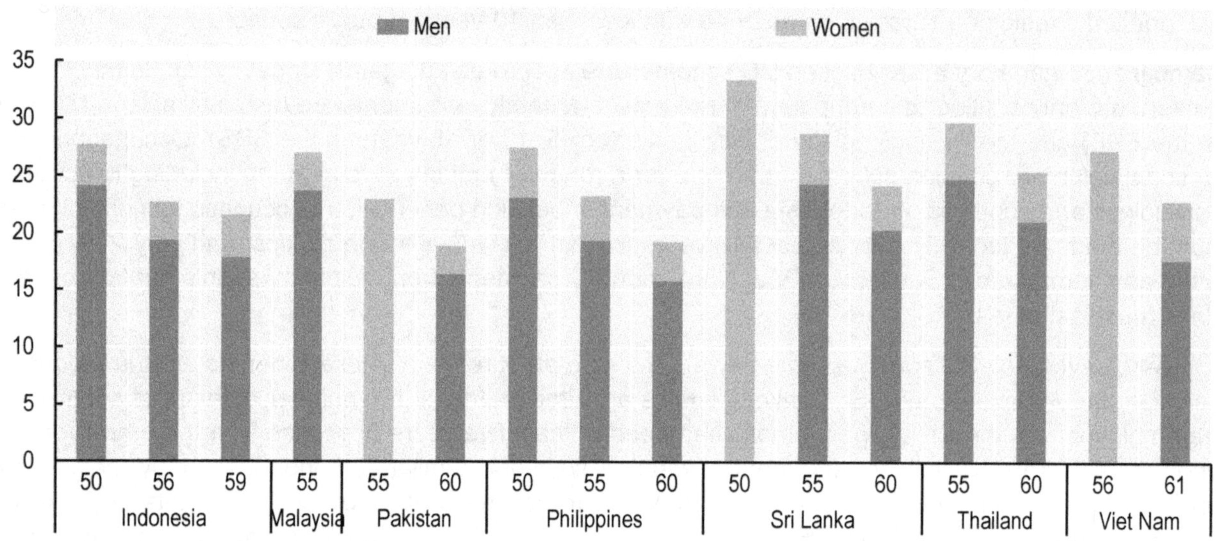

Note: Average life expectancy at different ages.
Source: United Nation's World Population Prospects 2024.

The replacement rates that private-sector employees entering the labour force in 2022 may expect to get after a full career vary across countries, genders and earnings levels. Figure 2.4 presents theoretical gross replacement rates from mandatory pension schemes for private-sector employees at three levels of earnings, for men and women (OECD, 2024[7]). Workers are assumed to contribute for a full career, defined as entering the labour market at age 22 and working until the normal age of retirement. As the normal age of retirement varies across countries, the length of the career also varies. For male average earners, gross replacement rates vary from 32% in Sri Lanka to 72% in the Philippines. They exceed the OECD average of 50.7% in Indonesia, the Philippines and Viet Nam.[20] In Indonesia, Malaysia, Pakistan and Sri Lanka, gross replacement rates are lower for women than for men, with the largest differences observed in Pakistan and Sri Lanka, where women can retire five years earlier than men. By contrast, in Viet Nam, women get a slightly higher gross replacement rate than men as their higher accrual rate during the initial years of participation more than compensates for their earlier retirement age (Table 2.5). Moreover, gross replacement rates decline significantly with earnings in Pakistan and Thailand. In Pakistan, this is because pension benefits are calculated based on the minimum wage instead of the actual wage earned by employees. In Thailand, the earnings cap in the benefit formula affects higher-income earners the most (Table 2.5).

Figure 2.4. Theoretical gross pension replacement rates for private-sector employees, by earnings, mandatory pension schemes

As a percentage of gross pre-retirement earnings

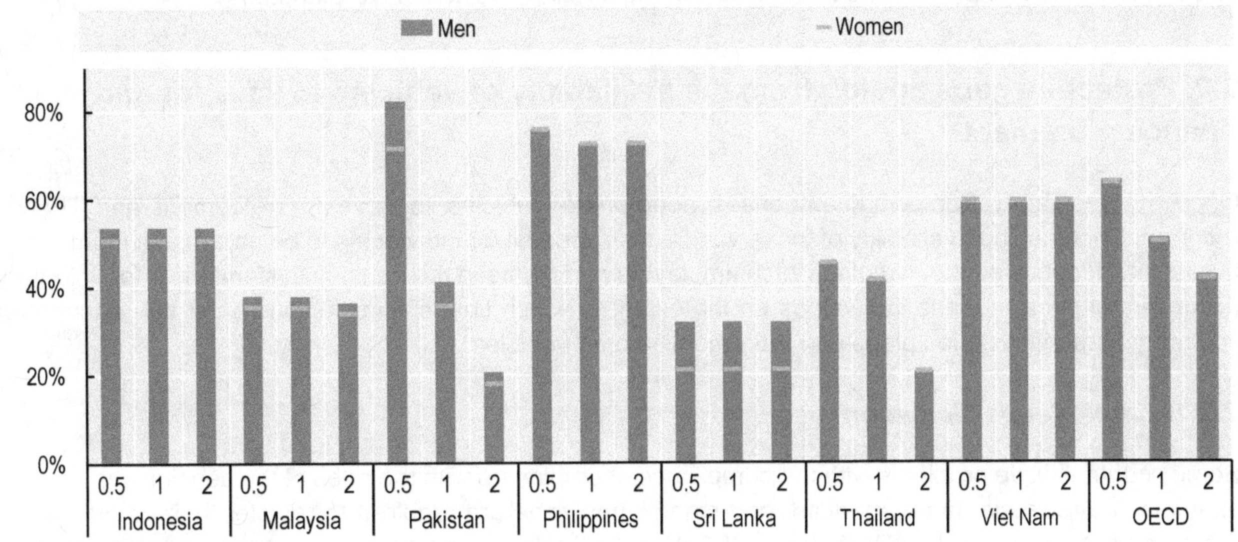

Note: 0.5 = half average earnings; 1 = average earnings; 2 = twice average earnings; OECD = OECD average.
Source: OECD (2024[7]), *Pensions at a Glance Asia/Pacific 2024*, OECD Publishing, Paris, https://doi.org/10.1787/d4146d12-en.

Replacement rates are likely to be higher for public-sector employees. Although theoretical gross replacement rates are not available for public-sector employees, the rules described earlier related to benefit formulas for DB pension schemes show that public-sector employees would receive higher pensions than private-sector employees after a full career in Indonesia, Pakistan, the Philippines and Thailand (Table 2.5). Besides, in Malaysia and Sri Lanka, public-sector employees are covered by a DB pension scheme that would provide a maximum gross replacement rate of 60% and 90%, respectively (Table 2.5). This is more than what the asset-backed DC scheme delivers for private-sector workers (Figure 2.4).

However, several countries are facing financial sustainability issues for tax-financed and PAYG DB pension schemes that may lead to an adjustment of the plan parameters, such as higher contribution rates, lower benefits and/or higher retirement ages. Several countries have accumulated public reserves for DB pension schemes. At the end of 2023, pension reserves represented 2% of GDP in Indonesia (Taspen – JP and BPJS – JP), 9% in Malaysia (JPA), 1% in Pakistan (EOBI), 10% in the Philippines (GSIS and SSS) and 11% in Thailand (SSF). However, given population ageing, relatively low contribution rates compared to benefits paid and low retirement ages, these reserves are expected to be depleted relatively soon. For example, in Indonesia, the benefit payments of the DB scheme for private-sector employees (BPJS – JP) are expected to exceed contributions from 2051 and the reserves are expected to last only until 2074. In Pakistan, the reserves of the mandatory PAYG DB scheme for private-sector employees (EOBI) are expected to be depleted around 2038. In the Philippines, the reserves of the PAYG DB schemes for public and private-sector workers (GSIS and SSS) are expected to be depleted by 2054 and 2058, respectively. In Thailand, the reserves of the PAYG DB schemes for private-sector workers (SSF Article 33 and Article 39) are expected to be depleted by 2054 (SSO, 2017[8]). In Malaysia, payments from the reserve fund of the mandatory pension scheme for public-sector employees (JPA) have started since 2018. Moreover, in Pakistan, provinces are transitioning from tax-financed DB to asset-backed DC schemes for public-sector employees as the liabilities of the DB schemes are no longer sustainable.

Similarly, the solvency of asset-backed occupational DB plans may not be fully guaranteed, putting at risk the delivery of pensions. For example, in Indonesia, employers are required to finance any funding deficit in their DB plans, but the requirements around how the liabilities are measured are very flexible. Hence, some pension funds use discount rates above the average rate of return. This may underestimate the value of liabilities and provide a distorted view of the funding position of DB plans.

2.2. Protection gaps arising from the availability of vehicles to save for and finance retirement

Once the regulatory framework authorises appropriate vehicles to save for retirement and finance retirement income, the availability of these vehicles is essential for individuals to be able to use them. Their availability depends on the extent to which employers participate in the pension system and offer voluntary occupational pension plans, as well as on the extent to which financial institutions enter the markets for voluntary personal pension plans and retirement income vehicles.

2.2.1. Employer participation

Some countries have problems with the compliance of employers with the rules of the pension system. For example, in Indonesia, large, medium, and small enterprises are required to register their employees in the mandatory asset-backed DC scheme (BPJS – JHT). However, enforcing companies to comply with this obligation is a challenge, especially for smaller ones. Hence, only around 38% of formal workers participate in a mandatory pension scheme (Taspen or BPJS). Similarly, compliance from small employers and self-employed workers is a challenge in the Philippines (SSS). At the end of 2024, self-employed and voluntary members represented 21% of all SSS members, even though self-employed and informal workers represent around one-third of total employment. In Pakistan, not all eligible companies are registered with the institution in charge of the PAYG DB scheme for private-sector employees (EOBI). In Viet Nam, the Vietnam Social Security submitted 417 files recommending prosecution against employers' evasion of social insurance contributions to the investigation agency between 2018 and 2023.[21] In 2023, around 67% of all enterprises and units in operation in Viet Nam participated in the mandatory pension scheme for employees and late and evading contributions amounted to VND 8 269 billion.

Employees in severance DB schemes financed through book reserves are at risk of not receiving their full benefits. In Indonesia, Pakistan and the Philippines, employers are not obliged to put money aside to finance the retirement severance benefits. Some employers may lack the resources to pay the benefits once they are due to retiring employees. Moreover, if the company goes bankrupt, employees may not receive any benefits. In Indonesia, less than 20% of employers are complying with their obligations to pay retirement severance to eligible employees, with mostly only large companies complying. Similarly, in the Philippines, there are many administrative cases of employees suing their employer for not having paid the retirement severance pay.

2.2.2. Provision of voluntary occupational pension plans

Employer provision of voluntary occupational pension plans tends to be low. For example, in Pakistan, the possibility for employers to offer occupational pension plans within the voluntary pension system (VPS) was only introduced in March 2024 and so far, no private-sector employer has offered such a plan. In the Philippines, only a few large employers offer occupational pension plans. In Thailand, less than 5% of employers are offering a provident fund (PVD) (ThaiPVD, 2022[4]). By contrast, in Indonesia, employers more commonly provide occupational pension plans to private-sector employees as these plans were introduced prior to mandatory pension schemes. This could be the case because employers offering occupational pension plans can use the assets from those plans to offset their severance liability on their balance sheet. However, since the introduction of the mandatory schemes for private-sector employees (BJPS – JP and JHT) in 2015, there has been a trend to close occupational pension plans. In 2015, 62% of companies provided an occupational pension plan (DPPK or DPLK), with 20% of these providing DB plans and 83% providing DC plans (Rosedewayani, 2017[9]). The number of DB pension funds has decreased from 164 in 2018 to 138 in 2023, and the number of DC pension funds has decreased from 44 to 36 (OJK, 2024[10]; OJK, 2022[11]). In 2022, 96 employer-provided occupational pension funds (DPPK) closed to new members.

2.2.3. Provision of voluntary personal pension plans

The provision of voluntary personal pension plans is concentrated in few providers. Table 2.7 shows the number of providers, the number of products they offer and the types of financial institutions that are allowed as providers. In the Philippines, there are only three administrators of PERA products, limiting the distribution of these products across the population. By contrast, Indonesia and Thailand have more than 20 providers of personal pension plans. There is usually a range of financial institutions that can apply for a license to provide personal pension plans.

Table 2.7. Providers of voluntary personal pension plans

	Type of plan	Number of providers	Number of investment products / pension funds	Types of providers allowed
Indonesia	DPLK	25		Banks, life insurance companies, asset managers
Malaysia	PRS	9	72	Banks, insurance companies, asset managers
Pakistan	VPS	16	45	Life insurance companies, asset managers, investment advisors
Philippines	PERA	3 administrators and 6 product providers	17	Banks, insurance companies, stand-alone trust corporations, securities brokers, investment houses, investment company advisers
Sri Lanka	Personal plans			Life insurance companies, banks
Thailand	RMF	21	374	Asset managers
Viet Nam	Supplementary voluntary pension	10		Life insurance companies, fund management companies

2.2.4. Provision of retirement income vehicles

The provision of lifetime retirement income vehicles by pension providers and insurance companies is limited in most countries. For example, in Indonesia, life insurance companies generally do not offer products paying lifetime income. A recent legislation allowed them to offer fixed-term annuities. In Malaysia, only fixed-term annuities are available. In Pakistan, only one insurance company is an active pension fund manager in the voluntary pension system (VPS) and offers an annuity plan. In the Philippines, insurance companies have shown interest in entering the market of voluntary personal pensions (PERA) and offer life annuity products, but such products are not available yet. In Sri Lanka, fixed-term annuities up to 20 years are available in the market.

2.3. Protection gaps arising from the population's use of the available vehicles to save for and finance retirement income

Even though individuals may have access to vehicles to save for and finance retirement income, they may not make use of available vehicles in a way that will lead to reaching their target retirement income. Individuals' behaviour may affect their participation in the different pension schemes, the amounts contributed to those schemes, the way the savings are invested, the amounts withdrawn before retirement and the way savings are used to finance the payout phase.

2.3.1. Participation rates

Mandatory pension schemes are far from reaching universal coverage. Figure 2.5 shows participation rates based on total and active membership in mandatory (Panel A) and voluntary (Panel B) pension schemes. Membership data from different pension schemes are summed up within each country, so the participation rates are likely to be an over-estimation as some individuals may be members of several pension schemes. While more than 60% of the working-age population in Malaysia and the Philippines are members of a mandatory pension scheme, participation rates fall to less than 30% in Sri Lanka, Thailand and Viet Nam, and to around 10% in Indonesia and Pakistan. In comparison, between 60% and 96% of the working-age population participates in mandatory pension schemes for private-sector employees in a sample of OECD countries (OECD, 2024[7]).

Figure 2.5. Participation rates based on total and active membership

As a percentage of the population aged 15 to 64

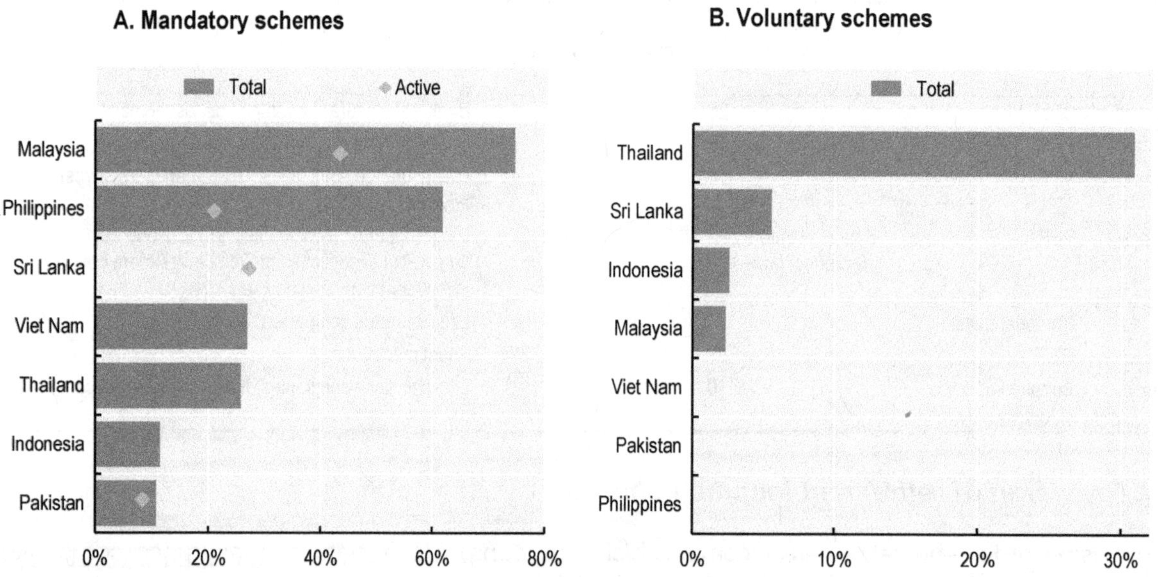

Notes: Data exclude members already drawing a pension. Data may include multiple counting as individuals may be members of several pension schemes, in particular for voluntary schemes. For Sri Lanka, data for the mandatory scheme for private-sector employees (EPF) refer to the number of active accounts, and total membership data are not available.
Source: OECD calculations based on national data sources on plan membership and working-age population.

Participation rates may be particularly low among women. The lower labour force participation of women (Figure 2.1) translates into a lower female representation in total membership. For example, in Indonesia (BPJS) and Pakistan (EOBI), women represent only 33% and 5% of all members, respectively, in the mandatory pension schemes for private-sector employees. By contrast, in Viet Nam, women represent about 55% of participants in the mandatory DB pension scheme (VSS).

Participation rates are even lower when considering active membership rather than total membership. Panel A of Figure 2.5 shows participation rates using both measures for Malaysia, Pakistan and the Philippines. In Malaysia, only around half of members of the mandatory pension scheme for private-sector employees (EPF) contribute to their plan at least once in any given year. In the Philippines, between 30%

and 50% of members of the mandatory pension scheme for private-sector workers (SSS) pay contributions from month to month. In Pakistan, out of 11.3 million members in the mandatory pension scheme for private-sector employees (EOBI), 7.4 million actively contribute. Lack of compliance from employers and self-employed workers, spells of unemployment, and transitions between formal and informal employment explain those gaps between members and contributors. For example, in the Philippines, private-sector workers do not earn additional entitlements in the mandatory pension scheme (SSS) under the DB formula between 10 and 20 years of participation. This may incentivise some workers to become informal once they have reached 10 years of participation in the scheme.

The uptake of voluntary pension schemes is also relatively low. Less than 6% of the working-age population participate in voluntary pension schemes in most countries (Panel B of Figure 2.5). Across OECD countries, participation rates in voluntary occupational and personal pension plans range from 3% to 60% of the working-age population (OECD, 2024[12]). Thailand stands out with a participation rate of 31%. This number may include multiple counting as individuals can have several pension plans. Additionally, the SSF Article 40 for informal workers already has a participation rate of 16% just by itself. This is due to a government COVID-19 relief package introduced in 2021 that provided a cash handout of THB 5 000 per month to workers registered with the SSF.[22] Many of these registered participants may not actively contribute.

Lack of awareness of the population and difficulties to claim tax incentives may explain the low uptake of voluntary pension schemes. Low levels of awareness of the population about voluntary pension schemes seem to be widespread across countries. Moreover, tax incentives may fail to encourage voluntary retirement savings in some countries. For example, for personal pension plans in Pakistan (VPS), employees can claim the tax credit on contributions through their employer subject to the filing of a tax return, while the self-employed need to undergo a complicated process for claiming tax benefits in their tax returns directly from the tax authority. As a result, self-employed workers only represent 7% of VPS members, even though these workers were one of the primary targets of the scheme. The process to claim the tax credit is similar in the Philippines for voluntary personal plans (PERA) and the self-employed only represent 15% of PERA members. In Viet Nam, amounts that can be deducted as voluntary pension contributions are different under the personal income tax system (VND 1 million per month) and the corporate income tax system (VND 3 million per month). As any contribution above VND 1 million is taxable for the individual, there is no incentive for them to contribute more than this amount, even though employers could contribute more as they have unused tax relief.

2.3.2. Level of voluntary contributions

Incomes vary significantly across different categories of workers, affecting their capacity to save for retirement. Women tend to earn less than men. For example, in Sri Lanka, the mean gross salary of female workers earning daily salaries was 56% of those of males in 2023 (LKR 17 527 for women and LKR 31 576 for men). Public-sector employees also tend to have higher earnings than private-sector employees. In Thailand, government employees had an average monthly wage of THB 21 000 in 2024, compared to THB 14 032 for private-sector employees. Moreover, there are also differences between formal employees, self-employed workers and informal workers. In Indonesia, the average monthly net income of regular employees was IDR 3 178 227 as of August 2023. The average net income of the self-employed was 63% that of regular employees, while the average net income of informal workers was less than 50% that of regular employees.

Individuals may contribute much less to their voluntary pension plans than the maximum allowed. There is little information about the level of contributions paid into voluntary pension schemes. In Malaysia, voluntary contributions to the mandatory pension scheme for private-sector employees (EPF) amounted to MYR 13.67 billion from 1.2 million contributors in 2024. This implies an average voluntary contribution of around MYR 11 400, much less than the annual limit of MYR 100 000. In the Philippines, a cumulative amount of PHP 491 million was paid into PERA accounts between December 2017 and December 2024. This translates into an average cumulative contribution of PHP 83 117 per member as of December 2024, or PHP 11 874 on average per member and per year.[23] This is much lower than the PHP 200 000 annual limit. In Thailand, informal workers insured under the SSF Article 40 can choose among three options for their insurance coverage. Option 1 covers sickness, disability and death. Option 2 covers the same risks as option 1 plus pension. Option 3 covers the same risks as option 2 plus child-allowance. The contribution rate is fixed under each option and increases with the number of risks covered. In 2021, 87% of those building pension entitlements (i.e. contributing under option 2 or option 3) contributed the lowest amount possible (i.e. THB 100 per month under option 2). This, combined with low contribution density (ILO, 2022[13]), translates into a modest lump sum at retirement. In Malaysia, 103 000 men have diverted part of their mandatory contributions (two percentage points of the employee's 11% contribution rate) to their spouse's account (I-sayang programme of the EPF) as of December 2024.

2.3.3. Investment strategies

The amount of assets accumulated in asset-backed pension plans remains modest. Figure 2.6 compares total investment as a percentage of GDP in the seven countries under review to that in OECD countries (Panel A) and other selected Asian jurisdictions (Panel B).[24] Except in Malaysia, where total investment in the mandatory pension scheme for private-sector employees (EPF) represented 62% of GDP at end-2023, total investment falls below 20% of GDP in the other countries. Pakistan, the Philippines and Viet Nam lag behind other selected jurisdictions in Asia, with total investment representing less than 0.5% of GDP at end-2023. One of the reasons for this low level of assets is that some of the asset-backed pension schemes have been introduced relatively recently in Indonesia (2015 for the BPJS), the Philippines (2021 for the mandatory DC component of the SSS), Pakistan (2005 for the VPS) and Viet Nam (2014 for voluntary supplementary pensions).

Figure 2.6. Total investment in asset-backed pension plans, end-2023

As a percentage of GDP

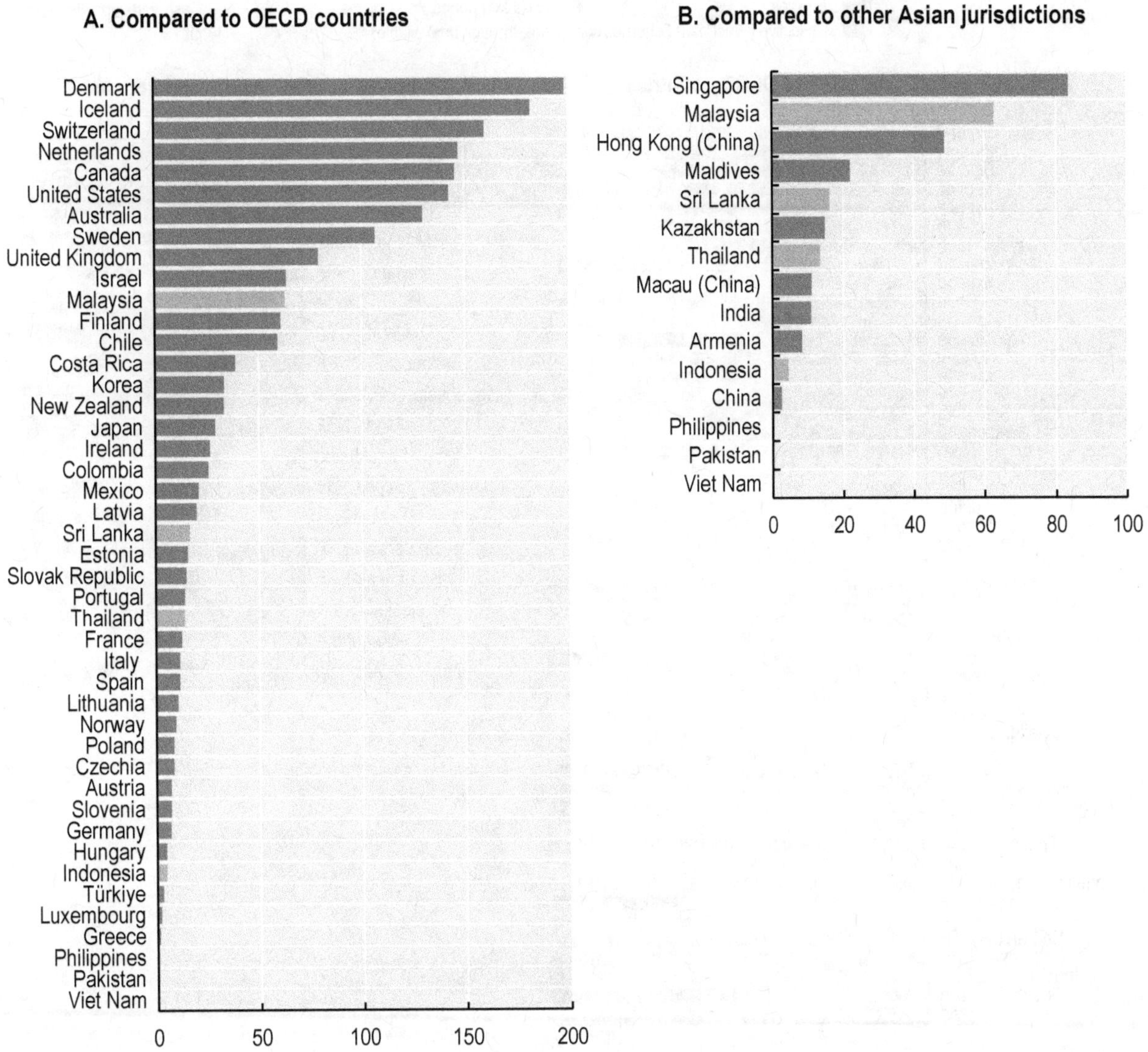

Note: Data for India refer to 2022.
Source: OECD Global Pension Statistics and national sources for Malaysia, Pakistan, the Philippines, Sri Lanka and Thailand.

Asset allocation strategies of asset-backed pension schemes tend to be conservative. Large allocations to bills and bonds are relatively common in Asia, as Panel B of Figure 2.7 shows. Within the bills and bonds allocation, domestic government bonds are predominant in Sri Lanka (more than 90% of total investment in the EPF and ETF schemes) and Indonesia (more than 65% of total investment in the BPJS schemes). Allocations to equities are relatively low compared to OECD countries, except in Malaysia, where the EPF invests 44% of its portfolio in equities (Panel A of Figure 2.7). Conservative investment strategies may lead to lower investment performance in the long term as countries become more developed and yields on domestic government bonds decline. Large allocations to domestic government bonds also create concentration risk as a default on those obligations would heavily affect the value of assets accumulated.

Figure 2.7. Asset allocation of asset-backed pension plans, end-2023

As a percentage of total investment

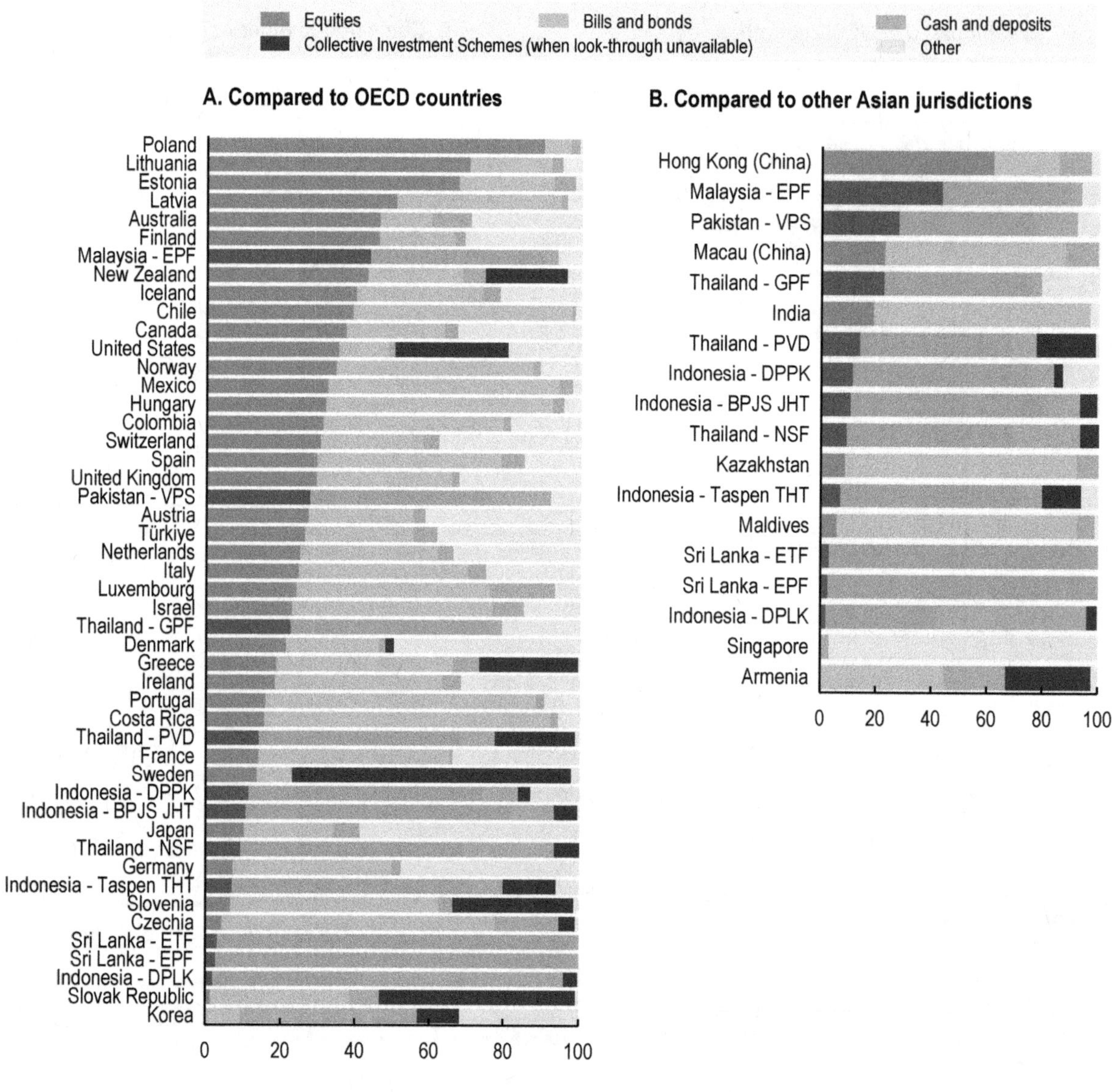

Notes: Data refer to end-2023 except for Malaysia, Pakistan and Thailand (end-2024). Data are not available for Viet Nam.
Source: OECD Global Pension Statistics and national sources for Malaysia, Pakistan, Sri Lanka and Thailand.

2.3.4. Early access to savings

Pension pots may be significantly reduced by the time individuals retire as they tend to use the different opportunities given to them to access their retirement savings before retirement. For example, in Indonesia, most of the assets in the DC component of the mandatory scheme for private-sector employees (BPJS – JHT) are withdrawn when members change or lose their job and only a small fraction of all claims is to members who have reached the age of retirement. Between 2016 and 2018, an average of 1.5 million people per month withdrew their savings from the scheme because they left their job. In Sri Lanka, since 2015, members of the mandatory pension scheme for private-sector employees (EPF) with at least 10 years of participation and LKR 300 000 in their account can withdraw 30% of their account balance for housing and medical expenses. A total of LKR 123.5 billion had been withdrawn by the end of 2022, with LKR 16.4 billion withdrawn by 27 278 members (about 1% of active members) in 2022 alone (EPF, 2023[14]). In Pakistan, around 10% of members of voluntary personal pension plans (VPS) withdraw funds before retirement on average each year (MUFAP, 2025[15]).

Individuals taking loans from their pension plans may fail to repay them in time and thereby receive a lower pension income. For example, in the Philippines, it is popular among members of the mandatory pension scheme for private-sector workers (SSS) to take loans as there is a strong borrowing culture in the country and the interest rate (10%) is usually lower than in the market. However, retiring members with outstanding debt must sometimes wait one or two years before receiving their full pension as deductions for loan repayment are taken from their pension income. In Sri Lanka, between 2013 and 2022, the mandatory pension scheme for private-sector employees (EPF) issued an average of 11 807 certificates of loan guarantees to the Department of Labour per year for the approval of housing loans amounting to LKR 5 690 million on average. However, around half of borrowers do not make their regular loan payments. On average, LKR 2 861 million was deducted from members' accounts per year and remitted to the relevant lending institutions to settle overdue loans between 2013 and 2022.

2.3.5. Payout options

Plan members tend to withdraw their retirement savings as a full lump sum when given this option at retirement. For example, in Pakistan, around 60% of members of voluntary personal plans (VPS) withdrew cash upon retirement in 2024 instead of entering a drawdown plan (MUFAP, 2025[15]). In Thailand, among the members of voluntary occupational pension plans (PVD) who retired in 2022, 81% took a lump sum, 16% remained invested (drawdown) and 3% received an annuity (ThaiPVD, 2022[4]). In Malaysia, there is also a general preference for lump sums among the members of the mandatory pension scheme for private-sector employees (EPF), but the provision of free financial advice has been reducing the proportion of people taking their savings as a single lump sum over time.

2.4. Main drivers of the financial protection gaps in retirement savings and policy options to addressing the gaps

This section first summarises the previous analysis by identifying the main drivers of the financial protection gaps in retirement savings using the experience of Indonesia, Malaysia, Pakistan, the Philippines, Sri Lanka, Thailand and Viet Nam. It then looks at approaches and policy options to addressing the gaps, distilling lessons learnt from those and other countries.

2.4.1. Drivers of financial protection gaps in retirement savings

Financial protection gaps in retirement savings mainly originate from the fact that many individuals fail to participate in pension and retirement savings schemes, and when they do, the benefits they can expect to receive may be insufficient or may not cover them for their entire lifetime in retirement.

Four main drivers explain why participation rates in mandatory pension schemes are below 60% of the working-age population in most countries (Figure 2.8). First, labour force participation rates are relatively low, especially among women, leaving a lot of individuals without access to mandatory pension schemes. Second, most mandatory pension schemes only cover formal employees. Informal and self-employed workers represent a large share of the employed population but are not covered by mandatory pension schemes, except in the Philippines. Third, certain private-sector employers are exempted from the obligation of registering their formal employees into mandatory pension schemes. Such exemptions tend to apply to smaller employers or to those operating in certain sectors (e.g. agriculture). Fourth, the level of compliance of employers and self-employed workers tends to be low.

Figure 2.8. Factors affecting participation rates in mandatory pension schemes

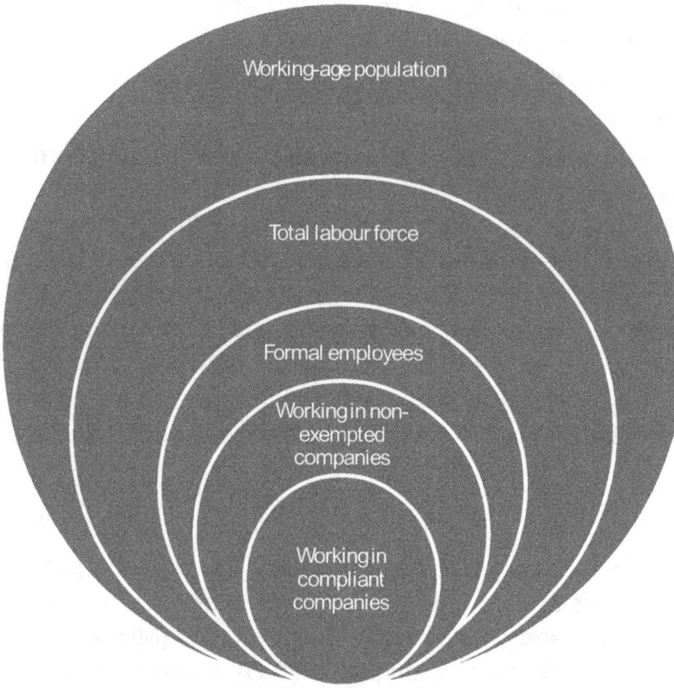

Additional drivers explain the low uptake of voluntary pension schemes. This uptake is below 6% of the working-age population in most countries. First, voluntary occupational pension schemes are not available in Malaysia, while their provision by employers is low or declining in the other countries. Therefore, only a small proportion of employees have access to voluntary occupational pension plans. Second, the number of providers of personal pension plans is relatively small in some countries (e.g. the Philippines), potentially limiting the distribution of these plans to a wide range of the population. Third, the population generally lacks awareness of the need to save for retirement and of the different vehicles available to them. Fourth, tax incentives fail to encourage some individuals to participate in voluntary pension schemes, in particular those with low or no income-tax liability and those who need to go through complex processes to claim tax relief. Fifth, employers and individuals may not be willing to voluntarily save more as mandatory contributions are already perceived to be high. Therefore, even though individuals have access to personal pension plans, many do not open a plan to save for retirement.

Among individuals participating in pension and retirement savings schemes, the retirement income they can expect to receive from these schemes may be inadequate. The drivers differ for DC and DB plans.

Short contribution periods and early access to savings are the two main drivers of lower-than-expected DC pension benefits. Pension benefits from DC plans are affected by the amounts contributed, the length of the contribution period, the investment strategy, and the amounts withdrawn before retirement. Contribution rates to mandatory asset-backed DC schemes may be in line with their role in the provision of retirement income in the different countries. In Malaysia and Sri Lanka, mandatory asset-backed DC schemes are the main source of retirement income for private-sector employees and their contribution rates are relatively high, at 23% in Sri Lanka (EPF and ETF) and 24% in Malaysia (EPF).[25] In the other countries, mandatory asset-backed DC schemes complement PAYG or tax-financed DB plans and contribution rates are therefore smaller. The length of the contribution period may not be long enough, however, to produce high enough pension benefits. Low retirement ages, currently between 50 and 61, reduce the length of the accumulation phase and imply that the accumulated assets need to finance a longer retirement period, in particular for women. As a result, expected gross replacement rates after a full career are lower than 40% in both Malaysia and Sri Lanka, despite contribution rates above 20% (Figure 2.4). The gross replacement rate even falls to 21% for women in Sri Lanka as they can retire 5 years earlier than men. Moreover, high levels of informality are likely to result in low contribution densities, as workers would stop contributing when switching from formal to informal employment. This would reduce expected benefits compared to a full career of contributions. Additionally, conservative investment strategies expose pension funds to concentration risk and may lead to lower performance in the long term as yields on domestic government bonds may decline as countries become more developed. Finally, pension assets may be significantly reduced by the time individuals retire as they tend to use the different opportunities given to them to access their retirement savings before retirement.

DB pension schemes may provide adequate retirement benefits, but several factors may undermine this. Indeed, with mandatory DB schemes providing yearly accrual rates at or above 2% in most countries, members can expect a replacement rate of minimum 60% after 30 years of service. However, benefit ceilings may significantly reduce expected benefits for higher-income earners. This is the case for example in Thailand for private-sector employees, where benefits are calculated based on capped earnings. Benefit ceilings will also affect an increasing share of plan members as they are usually not indexed to wage growth. In addition, the combination of high service period requirements and lack of portability between different pension schemes may reduce the proportion of members entitled to pension benefits. Indeed, a minimum of 10 to 25 years of service is required for members to become entitled to pension benefits. However, switching between formal and informal employment may reduce workers' ability to fulfil this requirement. Even among formal employees, lack of portability of pension rights from one employer to the next (e.g. DB severance schemes) or between pension schemes for public and private-sector employees may result in lost benefits for mobile workers. Finally, the financing of DB pensions may not always be secured. Indeed, pension benefits are not always aligned with the contributions paid and the age of retirement, and this imbalance combined with population ageing may result in the depletion of public reserves in a relatively short time horizon. Moreover, some employers may fail to pay occupational pension benefits or severance benefits because they did not put enough money aside to finance such benefits.

Lastly, many retiring individuals may lack protection from longevity risk. Only individuals fulfilling the retirement age and minimum service requirements are entitled to lifelong pensions from mandatory PAYG or tax-financed DB pension schemes. DB severance schemes only pay lump sums, while mandatory asset-backed DC schemes may offer a choice between lump sums and monthly instalments. Members of voluntary occupational and personal pension plans may be able to choose life annuities as payout option, but the provision of lifetime retirement income vehicles by pension providers and insurance companies is limited in most countries. Additionally, individuals tend to prefer lump sums over life annuities. Without lifelong payout options, individuals may risk outliving their resources or may underuse their resources to avoid running out of money.

2.4.2. Policy options to addressing financial protection gaps in retirement savings

This section provides policy options to addressing financial protection gaps in retirement savings based on the drivers discussed above. The main policy recommendations are to increase participation rates in mandatory and voluntary pension schemes, ensure sufficient contribution levels and contribution periods, align investment strategies with the long-term horizon of retirement savings, improve the portability of pension entitlements, limit access to savings before retirement and design payout options in line with people's needs in retirement.

Participation in mandatory pension schemes

Countries should increase the coverage of mandatory pension schemes to reduce the proportion of retirees relying on safety net programmes. The self-employed and private-sector employees working in small companies could be the first target to expand coverage. Existing exemptions may encourage some companies to use contractual workers instead of hiring employees or to remain below a certain size to avoid paying mandatory pension contributions, raising fairness issues regarding social protection (OECD, 2019[16]). The Philippines provides an example of a country with a mandatory pension scheme (SSS) covering all private-sector employees, domestic workers or household employees, self-employed workers and citizens working abroad. Viet Nam extended the coverage of its main pension scheme (VSS) to business managers and owners of registered household businesses, taking effect from 1 July 2025. Among OECD countries, the self-employed are covered by the same mandatory asset-backed pension scheme as employees in Colombia, Estonia, Iceland, Israel, Latvia and Sweden, for example (OECD, 2020[17]).

The tax authority could play a role in collecting mandatory pension contributions or enforcing compliance from the self-employed. Enforcing the payment of mandatory pension contributions from self-employed workers could be a challenge. If there is a reliable tax collection system, the tax authority could withhold mandatory contributions and channel them to pension funds, or identify workers and employers with delayed contribution payments. This would increase compliance. In Iceland for example, self-employed workers contribute to the mandatory occupational pension system once a year when they make their income declaration to the tax authority.[26] The tax authority is responsible for checking that contributions are paid and chases individuals when they fail to comply. In Chile, the self-employed pay their social security contributions in April of each year using the taxes withheld on their invoices during the previous year. These contributions cover the individual for the period from July of the year of payment of contributions until June of the following year. In Israel, the self-employed must pay pension contributions at the latest by the end of the tax year. However, a self-employed worker has the choice of making monthly payments, a one-off payment or periodic payments. After the income declaration process, the tax authority checks whether the individual has deposited the appropriate funds into a pension plan. If not, the tax authority sends a notice with the amount that needs to be paid within a certain date.

More generally, ensuring that the authorities have access to the information regarding enrolment and contributions is essential to their ability to enforce compliance. The Ministry of Labour in Sri Lanka has made efforts in this regard and has an internal data management system, which can automatically calculate notices for unpaid contributions to the mandatory pension scheme for private-sector employees (EPF). They also manage an online complaints system for employees to report if their employer has not paid their contributions. Nevertheless, they currently maintain separate databases with the Central Bank, who manages the administration and investment activities of the EPF. Both are working to harmonise the two databases to facilitate data sharing and minimise errors.

Countries could also take stronger measures to enforce compliance. For example, in Malaysia, employers failing to comply with their different obligations with respect to the mandatory pension scheme for private-sector employees (EPF) are subject to various penalties depending on the offense, ranging from bankruptcy actions, to seizure of assets, retention of passports of the company's directors, imprisonment and fines.[27] In Sri Lanka, the Ministry of Labour can take legal actions against employer non-compliance with EPF obligations if employers do not heed an initial warning. They have 68 regional offices with employees carrying out on-site inspections in 20 establishments per month to check employer compliance. In Viet Nam, late payment and evasion of contributions to the mandatory pension scheme for public and private-sector employees (VSS) are subject to penalties. Employers must pay the full amount of overdue contributions plus a fine of 0.03% per day. Administrative fines and non-monetary penalties are also possible.

Fines and sanctions can work to enforce compliance, however building partnerships with key players could also help. For instance, the SSS in the Philippines is building partnerships with different institutions to expand the number of private-sector workers participating in the mandatory pension scheme. Examples of partnerships include with the Commission on Filipinos Overseas[28] to reach contractual service workers, with the Cooperative Development Authority[29] to reach members of cooperatives, with the Philippine Crop

Insurance Corporation[30] to reach farmers and fisherfolk, and with the Angkas motorcycle taxi company[31] to reach platform workers. In Malaysia, the EPF has also engaged with various strategic partners to collaborate in helping members to save for retirement. These include the National Sports Council to reach athletes, the National Film Development Corporation Malaysia to reach workers in the creative industry and six platform providers to reach gig workers.

Ensuring incentives continue over time for workers to remain in formal employment and keep contributing to mandatory pension schemes may also increase compliance. In particular, the formula used in DB plans should avoid situations where additional years of contributions do not grant sufficient entitlements, as this may encourage workers to stop participating by switching from formal to informal employment. Adjusting the ceilings for earnings used in the DB formula in line with wage growth could help addressing the issue as it would avoid that pension rights lose relevance compared to workers' earnings. Setting fixed accrual rates could also ensure that any additional year of contribution earns the same additional pension rights.

Participation in voluntary pension schemes

Voluntary pension schemes are important to complement mandatory pension schemes. They allow people to reach higher pension income without forcing workers who cannot afford to contribute more to do so.

Countries could increase the role of employers in the provision of voluntary pension schemes. Employees value jobs offering access to an occupational pension plan, and so employers can use pensions to attract and retain employees, thereby reducing hiring and training costs (OECD, 2022[18]). Countries willing to increase access to voluntary pension plans among employees could consider reducing the barriers that may prevent employers to be involved in pension provision (OECD, 2022[18]). For example, Indonesia allows employers to convert their occupational pension plans from DB to DC with the aim of reducing the number of plan closures by reducing the risks borne by employers. In the Philippines, employers can contribute to the voluntary personal pension plan (PERA) of their employees, thereby removing the administrative burden of setting up their own occupational pension plan. Another approach is to promote pension arrangements pooling multiple employers (OECD, 2024[19]).

Countries could also implement automatic enrolment to raise participation rates in voluntary pension plans. Automatic enrolment has gained popularity since the late 2000s in the OECD (OECD, 2019[20]). It involves signing people up automatically to a pension plan and giving them the possibility to opt out, so participation remains voluntary. The policy harnesses the power of inertia and procrastination to increase the number of individuals joining a plan. Automatic enrolment is currently available in 10 OECD countries.[32] Depending on the country, workers are enrolled automatically by their employer or by the social security institute, and employers are not always obliged to contribute on behalf of employees staying in the plan. In New Zealand and the United Kingdom, all employers must enrol their eligible employees automatically into a pension plan and opt-out rates around 10% have resulted in significant increases in participation rates in voluntary pension plans (OECD, 2019[20]).

Additionally, countries could consider adjusting the design of their financial incentives. The OECD Recommendation for the Good Design of Defined Contribution Pension Plans recommends countries to "design financial incentives to maximise their impact on enrolment and contributions" (OECD, 2022[21]). Financial incentives provided through the tax system may not be the most appropriate when the goal is to encourage low-income earners to make voluntary pension contributions. Indeed, low-income earners may not have sufficient tax liability to fully enjoy tax deductions and tax credits, and they may not react to tax incentives due to a general lack of understanding of tax-related issues (OECD, 2018[22]). Non-tax financial incentives are better suited to target this population because they are not linked to the individual's tax liability and are directly paid into the pension account (OECD, 2018[23]). There are two categories of non-tax financial incentives, matching contributions and fixed nominal subsidies. Matching contributions are usually expressed as a percentage of the saver's own contribution, up to a limit. Fixed nominal subsidies are fixed payments and as such are more valuable to lower-income earners. Both types of incentives are only paid if the individual makes voluntary contributions. Among OECD countries, 10 provide state matching contributions and 7 provide state fixed nominal subsidies (OECD, 2024[2]). Malaysia and Thailand provide state matching contributions to encourage voluntary pension contributions in some of the schemes.

Education and communication efforts can also encourage individuals to contribute voluntarily to a pension plan by highlighting the importance of saving for the future and helping people to understand practically how they can go about contributing to a pension plan. To be effective, programmes should ideally be tailored to specific populations, in line with the OECD Recommendation on Financial Literacy (OECD, 2020[24]). There are several examples of successful communication and education efforts in OECD countries targeted at increasing the participation of women in pension plans, for example (OECD, 2021[25]). Sri Lanka has been successful at increasing participation in voluntary plans for the self-employed by employing individuals to specifically promote the plans and to enrol new members, with annual enrolees growing from 15 thousand per year to 50 thousand per year.

Contribution levels and duration

Countries may need to balance contribution rates, contribution periods and benefits to improve the financial sustainability of PAYG DB schemes. One approach is to increase contribution rates to mandatory pension schemes. For example, in Indonesia (BPJS – JP), Pakistan (EOBI) and Thailand (SSF Article 33), contributions are often insufficient to finance expected benefits from DB schemes, particularly in light of population ageing. Similarly, higher contribution rates to asset-backed DC schemes could increase expected benefits from these schemes (e.g. BPJS – JHT in Indonesia). Increases in mandatory contribution rates need to be gradual to allow contributors, employers and workers, to adjust to the change. For example, the contribution rate to the mandatory pension scheme for private-sector workers (SSS) in the Philippines increased gradually from 12% in 2019 to 15% in 2025, with the increase being shared between employers and employees. Nevertheless, any increase in mandatory contributions should be considered in light of individuals' capacity to save and existing voluntary contributions.

Some countries may also consider transitioning from non-contributory tax-financed pension schemes to contributory asset-backed pension schemes. Tax-financed pension schemes for public-sector workers exist in several countries. They impose a growing burden on public finances given population ageing. For example, in Thailand, government expenditures for the civil service pension have already increased significantly over the past decade, from around 0.8% of GDP in 2008 to around 1.3% in 2019 (World Bank, 2023[26]). As population ageing continues, the financial burden is expected to keep increasing, to reach 1.8% of GDP by 2035 and 2.4% of GDP by 2060 (World Bank, 2019[27]). One possible option is to transform tax-financed pension schemes into asset-backed pension schemes, with contributions being shared between employers and employees. This is what the different provinces of Pakistan are currently doing for their public employees. The KPK province is the first province that did it and it introduced a DC scheme for all employees joining on or after 7 June 2022.

Countries should also consider increasing retirement ages to allow workers to accumulate higher pension rights and assets along their career, thereby receiving higher pension benefits. Normal retirement ages currently vary from 50 to 61 years old across countries. This translates into a retirement period ranging from 16 to 33 years given current mortality rates (Figure 2.3). As life expectancy increases, the length of the retirement period is also expected to increase, putting DB pension plans under financial strain and reducing expected benefits from DC pension plans. As stated in the OECD Recommendation for the Good Design of Defined Contribution Pension Plans, individuals should be encouraged to contribute for longer by starting early and postponing retirement, in particular when life expectancy increases (OECD, 2022[21]). Retirement ages should increase gradually, like in Indonesia and Viet Nam. Retirement ages should also be harmonised across different mandatory pension schemes to avoid that individuals retire at the earliest possible age.

Moreover, countries should harmonise retirement ages between men and women. Women already expect to spend a longer time in retirement than men when retiring at the same age. Letting women retire earlier than men can put them at a disadvantage as they have less time to accumulate pension entitlements and whatever they have accumulated needs to finance a longer period. Most OECD countries have the same retirement age for both genders (OECD, 2021[25]).

Investment

Countries could introduce some investment choice for plan members in asset-backed DC schemes. The OECD Recommendation for the Good Design of Defined Contribution Pension Plans recommends investment choice, as it allows individuals to align their investment strategy with their preferences, investment horizon and level of risk tolerance (OECD, 2022[21]). However, existing minimum return guarantees should not be extended to all newly offered investment strategies, as individuals could then opt for the riskiest option knowing that they would not have to suffer in case of extreme negative scenarios. Furthermore, investment choice may be best suited for those with more investment knowledge or sufficient savings. In Malaysia, members of the mandatory pension scheme for private-sector employees (EPF) are only allowed to choose their own investments once their assets exceed a certain specified threshold. In addition to having sufficient savings, participants in the Central Provident Fund in Singapore must complete a Self-Awareness Questionnaire to ensure that they are conscious of their own capacity to choose investments appropriately and of the potential risks involved.

Countries should properly design a default investment strategy when introducing investment choice. Not all individuals are willing or able to make investment decisions. For these individuals, a default option is necessary. The OECD Recommendation for the Good Design of Defined Contribution Pension Plans argues that life-cycle investment strategies can be well suited as default options as they allow individuals to take risk when young while mitigating the impact of extreme negative events on accumulated assets as they get closer to retirement age (OECD, 2022[21]). However, many different glide paths are possible and other types of investment strategies may also be suitable. The OECD (2020[17]) provides a framework to assist countries to select the most appropriate default investment strategy given the role and features of the DC scheme, as well as the population's level of risk aversion. The mandatory asset-backed DC schemes for public-sector workers (GPF) in Thailand followed this framework to define the glide path of the default life-cycle investment strategy it introduced in 2023.

Moreover, countries should revise the investment framework of asset-backed pension schemes to allow for more diversification. The OECD Core Principles of Private Pension Regulation indicate that "investment regulation should be based on prudential principles such as diversification, dispersion, maturity and currency risk management" (OECD, 2016[28]). Minimum levels of investment in certain asset classes, such as domestic government bonds, should therefore be avoided as they could impede adequate diversification and increase concentration risk. Such investment floors may also prevent pension funds from investing more in riskier asset classes, such as equities and corporate bonds, even though such a strategy could be in the best interests of plan members given the long-term investment horizon of retirement savings. More investment in equities and corporate bonds would also help to develop local capital markets and to finance the economy.

Portability

Countries should consider transforming unfunded DB severance schemes into asset-backed pension schemes to allow workers to build up pension entitlements over their entire career when the schemes' objective is to help finance retirement.[33] There is no portability of severance benefits when changing employers. Workers get a lump sum corresponding to the number of years of service with their past employer, and in Indonesia and the Philippines, only the years of service with the last employer at the time of retirement count. In the latter case, employers may be reluctant to hire people close to retirement age to avoid having to pay severance benefits. Workers should be able to accumulate pension entitlements over their career instead of starting over whenever they change employers. In line with this, Indonesia is considering integrating the retirement severance pay into the mandatory schemes for private-sector employees (BPJS – JP and JHT), mandating employers to pay contributions to finance future benefits. In the Philippines, the Capital Markets Development Act of 2021 proposed the introduction of a new mandatory, fully funded and portable occupational pension system to substitute the retirement pay system. The bill received the Congress' approval but is still awaiting the Senate's approval. In Pakistan, the federal government and the Punjab province permit employers to offer voluntary personal pension plans (VPS) instead of gratuity or provident funds. This allows employees to carry with them the assets already accumulated when changing employers.

Countries should also ensure the portability of pension entitlements across different pension schemes. Most countries have separate mandatory pension schemes for public and private-sector workers. The rules of the schemes are different, usually granting higher pension entitlements to public-sector employees. Moreover, a minimum number of years of service is required to be entitled to pension benefits in DB schemes (Table 2.5). These aspects may impede labour mobility between the public and private sectors. In extreme cases, workers may lose some of their entitlements by switching between sectors. For example, in Thailand, someone working 23 years in formal employment, 9 years as a civil servant and 14 years as a private-sector employee, will only get a lump sum from the scheme for private-sector employees (SSF Article 33). One way to improve the portability of pension entitlements is to sum up the number of years of service under different schemes. This is the case for example in the Philippines, where individuals who have worked in the public and private sectors during their career but do not qualify for a pension under either of the pension schemes (they have less than 15 years of participation in the GSIS and less than 10 years of participation in the SSS) can add up their periods of contributions under both schemes to reassess eligibility. If the total period exceeds 10 years (the minimum requirement under the SSS), the individual receives a monthly pension at retirement from both the SSS and the GSIS proportionally to the contributions made under each scheme. Countries should also consider aligning the pension schemes for public and private-sector employees to promote equity and labour mobility, as is the case in Viet Nam. Most OECD countries have aligned or unified systems for civil servants and private-sector employees (OECD, 2016[29]).

Pension schemes should be able to efficiently administer members' accounts. In Pakistan, accounts with zero balances tend to remain open when members move to another pension fund manager or withdraw all their funds. Members should also be able to retain a single account within a pension scheme, even if taking a break from contributions or changing employers. In Sri Lanka, for example, people get a new account in the mandatory pension scheme for private-sector employees (EPF) every time they change employers. Streamlining accounts would help to prevent individuals from accumulating several small accounts and help to improve operational efficiencies thereby reducing costs for members.

Early access to savings

Countries should limit early withdrawals to individuals' exceptional hardship circumstances. Early withdrawal possibilities may increase participation in asset-backed DC pension schemes as they reassure savers that at least part of their money will be accessible in case of need. However, early access to retirement savings could jeopardise retirement income adequacy. A single withdrawal of 10% of accumulated assets could result in a 2% to 9% reduction in pension income depending on the age at the time of withdrawal (30, 45 or 60), with older people experiencing a larger impact as they have accumulated larger balances (OECD, 2020[17]). The OECD Recommendation for the Good Design of Defined Contribution Pension Plans states that "any early access to retirement savings should be a measure of last resort and based on individuals' specific hardship circumstances", such as financial hardship or severe illness (OECD, 2022[21]).

Countries could introduce emergency savings accounts within pension schemes to help individuals increase their financial resilience. Arrangements combining short-term and long-term savings could help individuals face emergencies without tapping into their retirement savings. Ideally, contributions to the emergency account should come in addition to the contributions to the retirement savings account to avoid reducing future retirement income. Malaysia recently introduced a three-pot system within the mandatory pension scheme for private-sector employees (EPF), much like Singapore. Prior to May 2024, 30% of the contributions went to the limited withdrawal account from which money could be withdrawn under specific circumstances, such as the purchase of a home, education, or for health issues, and 70% of the contributions went to the retirement account with no possibility for early withdrawals. Since May 2024, there is now a third account from which members can withdraw money at any time for any reason, subject to a minimum withdrawal amount of MYR 50. Of the total contributions, 75% now go to the retirement account, 10% to the limited withdrawal account and 10% to the fully flexible account. Therefore, more contributions are now locked in until retirement, while additional flexibility is provided to savers.

Payout options

Pension schemes representing the main source of retirement income should provide some level of lifetime income (OECD Recommendation for the Good Design of Defined Contribution Pension Plans) (OECD, 2022[21]). Mandatory asset-backed DC schemes only provide lump sum or drawdown payments, leaving individuals managing longevity risk by themselves. However, as these schemes are expected to be the primary source of retirement income for their members, they are likely to be used to finance individuals' essential spending in retirement. Payout options with a guaranteed lifetime income (i.e. lifetime annuities) are best suited for meeting essential spending needs because they ensure that the individual will have a certain level of income for life (OECD, 2024[30]). Nevertheless, there should be some flexibility for circumstances where this type of option may not be the most suitable, such as when individuals are in poor health or if they have not saved enough to obtain a meaningful level of lifetime income (OECD, 2024[30]).

Countries could consider establishing public annuity providers to service lifetime income payments for publicly provided pension plans, or to ensure the supply of lifetime income products when the private sector is unable to do so at a competitive price. Several OECD countries with mandatory or quasi-mandatory asset-backed pension schemes, such as Denmark, Lithuania and Sweden, rely on publicly established institutions to provide lifetime income payments to members in retirement. Other countries, such as Croatia and Singapore, have public annuity providers that operate alongside private providers to promote competition in the market, thereby ensuring the availability of cost-efficient products. Public annuity providers should have robust risk management frameworks in place to manage risk exposures and ensure that they will have sufficient capital to make the lifetime payments to their members. Absent such requirements, the government would effectively act as the backstop of the provider in case of any solvency problems, which would unfairly shift the cost and risk of providing lifetime income products to the taxpayers.

Countries could also consider allowing non-guaranteed lifetime income options. Non-guaranteed lifetime income options provide longevity protection to retirees while limiting the risk exposure to providers, which could help to promote the availability of lifetime income options for pensioners. These types of products pool the longevity risk of participants and provide regular income payments, but unlike regular lifetime annuities, the level of the income is adjusted up or down depending on the actual investment and longevity experience of the plan. As such, it is the participants of the plan who collectively bear the investment and systemic longevity risks, while still being protected from idiosyncratic longevity risk of living longer than the average life expectancy. In addition, as payments are not guaranteed, banks and asset managers could offer such products, not only life insurance companies (OECD, 2022[31]).

Finally, countries could encourage and facilitate the provision and uptake of personalised guidance. Guidance at retirement aims to engage individuals in their decision regarding how to finance retirement with their accumulated savings and to give them the necessary information and tools to make the decision themselves (OECD, 2024[30]). Personalised guidance not only presents and explains the different options, but it also provides suggestions to individuals regarding which option is likely to be appropriate given their general characteristics. Financial advice goes even further as it aims to indicate the most suitable payout options given the individual's specific needs and circumstances. As such, it is more resource intensive than personalised guidance (OECD, 2024[30]). Malaysia set up a financial advice service for members of the mandatory pension scheme for private-sector employees (EPF) in 2014. The Relationship & Advisory (RA) programme, previously known as the Retirement Advisory Service (RAS), is free of charge for EPF members and aims to guide them at different life stages to assess their current financial situation and future needs, define financial goals and strategies to achieve them, plan for retirement and manage their finances after retirement. Since its launch in July 2014, the programme has supported over 542 000 EPF members (out of 8.8 million active members) through face-to-face advisory sessions conducted by certified RA officers. Additionally, RA officers have conducted financial literacy talks for the public, reaching an estimated audience of approximately 1.5 million people since February 2016. The programme has been successful at encouraging members not to withdraw all their savings as a lump sum and to draw down their savings more gradually over time.

References

EPF (2023), *Employees' Provident Fund Annual Report 2022*, https://epf.lk/wp-content/uploads/2024/05/Annual-report-English-2022.pdf. [14]

ILO (2022), *Thailand Social Protection Diagnostic Review: Review of the pension system in Thailand*, https://www.ilo.org/asia/publications/labour-markets/WCMS_836733/lang--en/index.htm. [13]

Kementerian Keuangan Republik Indonesia (2024), *Harmonization of Pension Programs in Indonesia: Initiative to Improve Old-age Protection and Advancing Public Welfare - DRAFT*. [33]

MUFAP (2025), *MUFAP 2024 Yearbook*, https://mufap.com.pk/Upload/WebDoc/Communication/Yearbook3070.pdf. [15]

OECD (2024), *Annual Survey of Investment Regulation of Pension Providers 2024*, https://www.oecd.org/content/dam/oecd/en/topics/policy-sub-issues/asset-backed-pensions/2024-Survey-of-Investment-Regulation-of-Pension-Providers.pdf. [3]

OECD (2024), *Annual survey on financial incentives for retirement savings: Country profiles 2024*, OECD Publishing, Paris, https://doi.org/10.1787/16d0283c-en. [1]

OECD (2024), "Assessing the design of financial incentives for retirement savings in OECD countries", in *OECD Pensions Outlook 2024: Improving Asset-backed Pensions for Better Retirement Outcomes and More Resilient Pension Systems*, OECD Publishing, Paris, https://doi.org/10.1787/51510909-en. [2]

OECD (2024), "Designing the payout phase for defined contribution pensions to better meet financial needs in retirement", in *OECD Pensions Outlook 2024: Improving Asset-backed Pensions for Better Retirement Outcomes and More Resilient Pension Systems*, OECD publishing, Paris, https://doi.org/10.1787/51510909-en. [30]

OECD (2024), "Improving access to asset-backed pension plans through arrangements pooling multiple employers", in *OECD Pensions Outlook 2024: Improving Asset-backed Pensions for Better Retirement Outcomes and More Resilient Pension Systems*, OECD Publishing, Paris, https://doi.org/10.1787/51510909-en. [19]

OECD (2024), *Pension Markets in Focus 2024*, OECD Publishing, Paris, https://doi.org/10.1787/b11473d3-en. [12]

OECD (2024), *Pensions at a Glance Asia/Pacific 2024*, OECD Publishing, Paris, https://doi.org/10.1787/d4146d12-en. [7]

OECD (2022), "How best to involve employers in the provision of asset-backed pension arrangements", in *OECD Pensions Outlook 2022*, OECD Publishing, Paris, https://doi.org/10.1787/20c7f443-en. [18]

OECD (2022), "Policy lessons for the design, introduction and implementation of non-guaranteed lifetime retirement income arrangements", in *OECD Pensions Outlook 2022*, OECD Publishing, Paris, https://doi.org/10.1787/1f1cdca9-en. [31]

OECD (2022), "Recommendation of the Council for the Good Design of Defined Contribution Pension Plans", *OECD/LEGAL/0467*, https://legalinstruments.oecd.org/en/instruments/OECD-LEGAL-0467. [21]

OECD (2021), "Gender implications of the design of retirement savings plans", in *Towards Improved Retirement Savings Outcomes for Women*, OECD Publishing, Paris, https://doi.org/10.1787/f7b48808-en. [25]

OECD (2020), "Recommendation of the Council on Financial Literacy", *OECD/LEGAL/0461*, https://legalinstruments.oecd.org/en/instruments/OECD-LEGAL-0461. [24]

OECD (2020), "Retirement savings and old-age pensions in the time of COVID-19", in *OECD Pensions Outlook 2020*, OECD Publishing, Paris, https://doi.org/10.1787/67ede41b-en. [17]

OECD (2020), "Selecting default investment strategies", in *OECD Pensions Outlook 2020*, OECD Publishing, Paris, https://doi.org/10.1787/67ede41b-en. [5]

OECD (2019), "Are funded pensions well designed to adapt to non-standard forms of work?", in *Pensions at a Glance 2019: OECD and G20 Indicators*, OECD Publishing, Paris, http://10.1787/b6d3dcfc-en. [6]

OECD (2019), "Non-standard forms of work and pensions", in *Pensions at a Glance 2019: OECD and G20 Indicators*, OECD Publishing, Paris, https://doi.org/10.1787/b6d3dcfc-en. [16]

OECD (2019), "The role of automatic enrolment schemes in enhancing funded pension systems' inclusiveness and retirement income adequacy", in *Financial Markets Insurance and Pensions: Inclusiveness and Finance*, https://www.oecd.org/content/dam/oecd/en/publications/reports/2019/01/financial-markets-insurance-and-pensions-2019_04d48a68/6e9e00ea-en.pdf. [20]

OECD (2018), "Are financial incentives effective tools to increase participation in and contributions to retirement savings plans?", in *Financial Incentives and Retirement Savings*, OECD Publishing, Paris, https://doi.org/10.1787/9789264306929-en. [22]

OECD (2018), "Policy guidelines to improve the design of financial incentives to promote savings for retirement", in *Financial Incentives and Retirement Savings*, OECD Publishing, Paris, https://doi.org/10.1787/9789264306929-en. [23]

OECD (2016), "Civil service pensions: Toward a unified system with the private sector", in *OECD Pensions Outlook 2016*, OECD Publishing, Paris, https://doi.org/10.1787/pens_outlook-2016-en. [29]

OECD (2016), *OECD Core Principles of Private Pension Regulation*, OECD Publishing, Paris, https://doi.org/10.1787/c950bb36-en. [28]

OJK (2024), *A Glance of Indonesia Pension Program*. [10]

OJK (2022), *Statistik Dana Pensiun 2022*, https://ojk.go.id/id/kanal/iknb/data-dan-statistik/dana-pensiun/Documents/Pages/Buku-Statistik-Dana-Pensiun-2022/Buku%20Statistik%20Dana%20Pensiun%202022.pdf. [11]

Rosedewayani, S. (2017), *Fiscal and other incentives for pension and saving schemes in Indonesia*, https://www.ojk.go.id/id/kanal/iknb/berita-dan-kegiatan/info-terkini/Documents/Pages/OJK-dan-World-Bank-Gelar-Indonesia-Pension-Conference/Session3_Pension%20Day_Fiscal%20and%20Other%20Incentive_Santhi%20Devi%20WTW_v4.pdf. [9]

SSO (2021), *Annual Report 2021*, https://www.sso.go.th/wpr/main/privilege/%E0%B8%A3%E0%B8%B2%E0%B8%A2%E0%B8%87%E0%B8%B2%E0%B8%99_sub_category_list-label_1_130_716. [32]

SSO (2017), *Annual Report 2017*, https://www.sso.go.th/wpr/main/privilege/%E0%B8%A3%E0%B8%B2%E0%B8%A2%E0%B8%87%E0%B8%B2%E0%B8%99_sub_category_list-label_1_130_716. [8]

ThaiPVD (2022), *Provident Fund Performance Report For the Second Half of 2022*, https://www.thaipvd.com/document/%E0%B8%82%E0%B9%89%E0%B8%AD%E0%B8%A1%E0%B8%B9%E0%B8%A5%E0%B8%AA%E0%B8%96%E0%B8%B4%E0%B8%95%E0%B8%B4. [4]

World Bank (2023), *Thailand public revenue and spending assessment: Promoting an inclusive and sustainable future*, https://www.worldbank.org/en/country/thailand/publication/th-prsa. [26]

World Bank (2019), *Thailand: Staff report for the 2019 Article IV Consultation*, https://www.imf.org/en/Publications/CR/Issues/2019/10/07/Thailand-2019-Article-IV-Consultation-Press-Release-Staff-Report-and-Statement-by-the-48724. [27]

Notes

[1] This chapter distils experiences and policy lessons from Indonesia, Malaysia, Pakistan, the Philippines, Sri Lanka, Thailand and Viet Nam. It describes the rules of the pension system of Viet Nam as specified in the 2024 Social Insurance Law, which was passed in June 2024 and is effective as of 1 July 2025.

[2] This proportion includes public-sector employees and the armed forces and military.

[3] The informal sector is defined as industrial units that are not registered, companies with less than 10 employees and companies with no regular employees. It does not include the agricultural sector.

[4] This proportion includes public-sector employees (9% of total employment).

[5] OECD calculations based on national labour force surveys referring to various periods between 2020-21 and Q2 2024.

[6] In Viet Nam, providers may require individuals to commit to contribute for a minimum period, e.g. five or ten years.

[7] It is common practice in Indonesia for employers to use occupational pension plans to finance their mandatory severance benefits.

[8] In the Philippines, it is not mandatory for employers to put money aside in a sperate fund to finance benefits from occupational pension plans. However, most employers do.

[9] Around 10% of SSS members contributed based on the minimum salary credit in 2024.

[10] Lump sums above that threshold are taxed at 5% and annuities are taxed at the individual's marginal income tax rate.

[11] Overseas Filipinos can contribute twice as much as domestic workers (PHP 400 000 instead of PHP 200 000) as they are less likely to be able to use the tax credit.

[12] Only contributions up to 20% of taxable income are considered for the tax credit.

[13] The income threshold below which individuals do not pay personal income tax varies from 82% of the average wage in Thailand to 352% of the average wage in Sri Lanka.

[14] The SSF Article 40 has three contribution options. Under option 1, members contribute THB 70 and the government contributes THB 30 per month. Under option 2, members contribute THB 100 and the government contributes THB 50 per month. Under option 3, members contribute THB 300 and the government contributes THB 150 per month. Only options 2 and 3 cover old-age benefits, as well as other benefits such as healthcare, disability and death benefits depending on the chosen option.

[15] Following the government's privatisation policy since the 1990s, the issuance of government securities has declined and the EPF has been exempted from the minimum investment requirement.

[16] In Malaysia, contributions to the mandatory asset-backed DC scheme for private-sector employees (EPF) are split between three accounts for members under the age of 55: 75% of the contributions are

paid into the retirement account and cannot be withdrawn before age 55, 15% are paid into the well-being account and can be withdrawn under selected conditions, and 10% are paid into the flexible account and can be withdrawn for any purpose.

[17] Men with less than 20 years of participation, but at least 15, are entitled to a monthly pension equal to 40% of their average salary with 15 years of participation (2.25% yearly accrual rate) and accrue 1% for each additional year between 15 and 20 years (thereby equalling 45% of average salary with 20 years of participation).

[18] Pension benefits may be paid as a single lump sum under specific conditions. These conditions are different for employer pension funds (DPPK) and financial institution pension funds (DPLK).

[19] In Indonesia, the benefit varies between 1.75 to 25.75 times the last salary depending on service duration. In Pakistan, the benefit is equal to the last pay or the highest pay over the past 12 months multiplied by the number of years of service. In the Philippines, the benefit is equal to one-half month salary multiplied by the number of years of service, with one-half month salary including 15 days of pay, 5 days of service-incentive leave and one-twelfth of the 13th month pay. In Sri Lanka, the benefit is equal to 15 days of wages for each completed year of service.

[20] Based on a more realistic assumption of 32 years of participation (instead of 43 years), the Indonesian Ministry of Finance calculates a replacement rate from the BPJS schemes of 27.4% (Kementerian Keuangan Republik Indonesia, 2024[33]).

[21] International Social Security News

[22] The number of informal workers insured under the SSF Article 40 increased significantly from 3.5 million in 2020 to 10.7 million in 2021 (SSO, 2021[32]).

[23] The average contribution per year is slightly higher for overseas Filipino workers, at PHP 14 892. This is in line with their higher annual contribution limit (PHP 400 000).

[24] Data do not include investment in public pension reserve funds that are meant to help finance future expenditures from PAYG and tax-financed pension schemes.

[25] For Malaysia, the contribution rate of 24% only applies to Malaysians and permanent resident workers under the age of 60 and earning up to MYR 5 000 per month. Lower contribution rates apply for employees earning more than MYR 5 000 per month and for employees aged 60 and above.

[26] Self-employed workers can pay more regular contributions if they so wish. This flexibility is important as some self-employed workers do not have a regular income stream on which to collect monthly contributions.

[27] Employer: Compliance with Acts to Contribute - KWSP Malaysia

[28] CFO partners with SSS to provide benefits for contractual workers | Philippine News Agency

[29] SSS partners with CDA to strengthen social security coverage and protection among members of cooperatives | Republic of the Philippines Social Security System

[30] Philippine pension SSS inks deal to extend pension coverage to farmers, fisherfolk | Asia Asset Management

[31] SSS, Angkas tie up to provide social security benefits for motorcycle taxi riders - Manila Standard

[32] Canada, Germany, Italy, Lithuania, New Zealand, Poland, the Slovak Republic, the Republic of Türkiye, the United Kingdom and the United States.

[33] If not going through a transformation, countries should at least consider removing the possibility for employers to use assets in occupational pension plans to fully or partially offset their obligations under DB severance schemes, as is the case in Indonesia and the Philippines. As an example, Hong Kong (China) abolished the MPF offsetting arrangement in 2022. Employers can no longer use accrued benefits derived from employers' mandatory contributions to the Mandatory Provident Fund (MPF) to offset employees' severance payment and long service payment in respect of the years of service starting from 1 May 2025. In parallel, the Labour Department launched a 25-year subsidy scheme to ease the additional financial burden on employers.

www.ingramcontent.com/pod-product-compliance
Lightning Source LLC
LaVergne TN
LVHW060453061126
851857LV00016B/1813